Shiny Happy People

no man is lonely while eating spaghetti.
ROBERT MORLEY

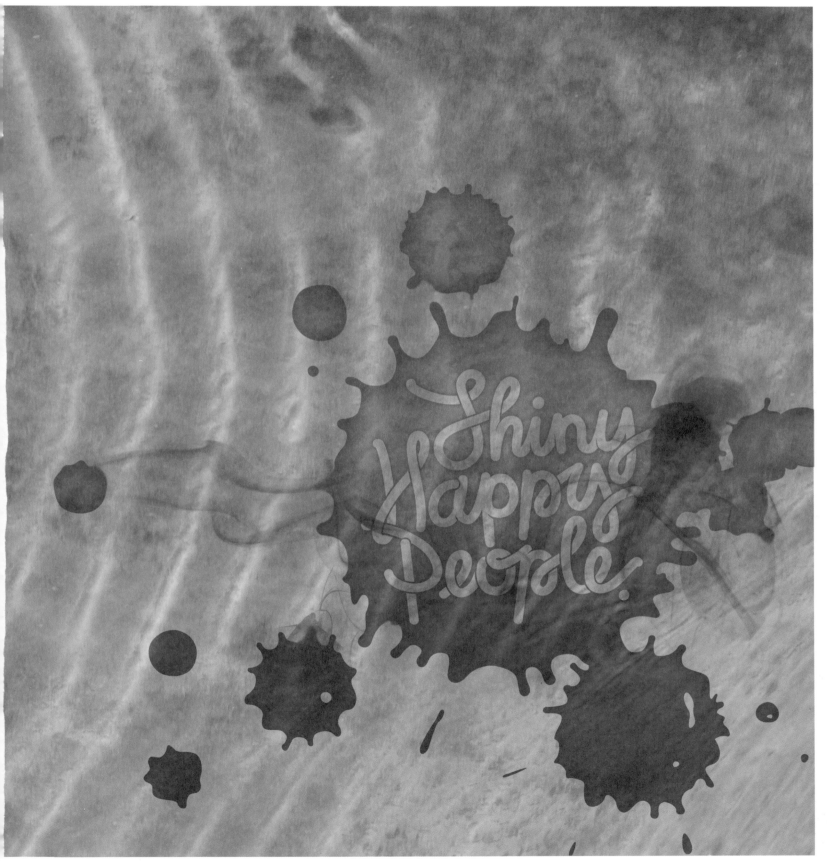

Shiny Happy People

IN AN EVER-CHANGING WORLD, UPON WHICH MY FAMILY IS WIDELY SCATTERED, IT'S COMFORTING TO KNOW THAT MY FRIENDS ARE MY NEW FAMILY. THEIR HOMES ARE THE PLACES WHERE I FIND SOLACE AT THE END OF A WORKING DAY. I'LL POP IN FOR AN ICE-COLD BEER, STAY FOR A CASUAL CHOW, AND THEN THE HOURS MELT AWAY - THAT'S USUALLY THE WAY IT GOES. WHETHER IT'S WITH MY KIDS IN TOW OR ON MY LONESOME, THERE'S ALWAYS ROOM AT THE KITCHEN COUNTER, AROUND THE BRAAI, OR EVEN AT THE STOVE, WHERE COOKING BECOMES A SHARED JOY.

Friends are my constant comfort and joy - and paging through this book's proofs before it went to print, I realised just how flipping stylish their personal dens are; from the minimalist black Bauhaus box Greg and Roché live in, to the pimped-out retro pad of Nikki and Brandon, or the über-stylish townhouse of my mate Cobra, each of my friends' homes (some old, some new - like the friends) has its own personal style. And, like it or dislike it, that style permeates every inch of their living space.

My friends can also cook - and I mean really cook. Maybe they're all genetically blessed, to be able to cater, entertain, design, decorate - even laugh - with such natural flair. Of course, any friend of mine is a friend of yours; so if you're feeling exotic, feel free to dip into gorgeous Ruth and Rowan's Algerian couscous sensation or Jeannette's Danish feast. If, somewhat curiously, you feel an itch to drag out and don your dusty lederhosen, then Nikki's German bratwurst (and the best potato salad I have ever tasted) should be right up your autobahn. Want to impress your own friends? Roll up your sleeves and attempt Roche's squid ink ravioli with a to-die-for prawn filling. If you're knackered and just in the mood for something simple but delicious, try Alex's Iranian version of a chicken mayo salad. What else...oh yes: there's one reason you're guaranteed to love this book, and that's Cobra's chimichurri sauce and steak. Cobra and I once hit the steakhouses of Buenos Aires together (one of the hippest cities on this planet - a must-see) and this is the version we brought back, for you to take and make your own.

But wait, as the ad people say, there's more... Greg's quail just has to be taste-tested, while from one of my favourite peeps in the world, the savvy and sexy Catherine, comes a banana buttermilk pancake recipe so good you'll want to marry her.

Oh flip, I nearly forgot - he'd kill me if I neglected to mention his love and joy - Russel's peri-peri prawns, made in a newly built wood-fired oven (which he actually talks to). Russel would be a much thinner shadow of himself without gorgeous wife Camilla by his side (please try her renaissance chicken liver pâté; you can't go wrong). Then there's the man who taught me how to cook Italian, the Marcella way. Any dish of Graeme's is flawless and will win you brownie points, should you choose to make it.

But what is eating without drinking? You see, sometimes we men do drink pink drinks... such as Brandon's (A.K.A. Bond, or as I call him, Bondage) pink martini - which would go so perfectly ("Ooh La La") with one of Sue's famous French desserts.

So that's it. An informal roll call of my legendary friends and their undeniable culinary skills (even if I am biased). And yet... I can't go without mentioning the one person who really should not have been in this book, because (oh the horror!) the girl just can't cook. That's Tiff. Still - ye gods! - can she ever mix a drink, turn up the volume, sing outrageously badly, roller-skate across her lounge floor, trip over nothing and talk very loud and very fast... and that's why I love Tiffany. She's SHINY AND HAPPY. Anyway, her husband Simon can cook and bake like a master, so Tiff's bacon is saved.

Thanks for reading and I hope you enjoy making friends with colour, food, décor and most of all, my friends.

"Schweet" Neil
ZA LOCAL

do not be afraid of cooking, as your ingredients will know, and misbehave.

- FERGUS HENDERSON

Tiff
AND
Simon

PAGE 6

Alex
AND
Jeannette

PAGE 154

Catherine

PAGE 56

Nikki
and
Brandon

PAGE 104

Lucie
Sue
AND
Tom

PAGE 32

Clinton
AKA
'COBRA'
PAGE 234
Rowan
Ruth
AND
Sophie
PAGE 192
Graeme
PAGE 82
Greg
AND
Roché
PAGE 212
Kate
PAGE 174
Russel
AND
Camilla
PAGE 130

sweet potato, aubergine & beetroot crisps
hedgehog loaf
half & half rye and wholewheat bread
boiled leg of lamb
bouillabaisse
authentic moussaka
kebab meatballs
chilli crab
orange chiffon cupcakes with granadilla frosting

Tiff and Simon
SUMMERVELD KZN

MODEL BOSS, TIFFANY PRIOR, AND ENTREPRENEUR, SIMON HEMINGWAY, MAKE THE MOST OF THEIR SHONGWENI HIDEAWAY IN KZN. SET AMIDST THE HORSEY COUNTRYSIDE, IT'S THE PERFECT SPOT FOR TIFF TO ESCAPE FROM THE FASHION WORLD AND EMPTY HER HEAD WHILE GALLOPING THROUGH THE VALLEYS. SIMON, HOWEVER, FINDS IT THE PERFECT BASE FROM WHICH TO EXPLORE ORGANIC PRODUCERS IN THE AREA FOR HIS THRIVING NEW CHUCK & BOB'S DELIVERY SERVICE.

I have eaten more meals than I can count with Tiff… bistros and workers' cafes in Paris, gastro pubs on the Thames, *Katz Deli* in downtown NYC, Michelin-starred Chinese at *Yauatcha* in London and dodgy Chinese in my hometown of Durban.

However, none can top the countless meals shared around our own tables at home. Simon is a consummate cook, never scared to try something new (like pork cooked in milk anyone? Or a sourdough yeast culture started with grapes?). It's not only this constant search for newness that makes the meals memorable, but also the fact that their home in Shongweni is warm, welcoming and inviting to big people, kids and of course, the dogs. Life for Tiff changed one fateful day while I was travelling

with her. Simon called to tell her their Durban home was sold and they were moving to Shongweni (about 40 minutes from Durban, in the countryside). It was all drama, drama, drama… but 2 years down the line, there is a new respect for country living and a beautiful home that Simon built for them. Riding crops have replaced the stilettos and the Little Black Numbers have been substituted for comfortable weekend wear. Not that it's all slow food and sunshine… life is still hectic for both Simon and Tiff, so when we do get time together, it's uptime in the kitchen with everybody helping out, and downtime at the tables with everyone tucking in. Simon admits that he doesn't even like crab or bouillabaisse, but he makes them because they're his wife's favourites. Now that's real kitchen love.

1. A FRANKFURT AIRPORT SPECIAL 2. FAMILY PICTURES GOING BACK GENERATIONS 3. GUESS TIFF'S FAVOURITE COLOUR… 4. THE GUEST(S) BATHROOM 5. TIFF & SIMON'S MAIN BATHROOM 6. QUIRKY TOWEL HOLDERS FROM THE SPACE 7. TIFF'S FAVOURITE FLOWERS 8. THEIR BABY – TIA, AKA OINK 9. THEY LOVE TO SPLASH OUT ON MATES 10. BIRTHDAY GIFT FROM DESIGN DUO, GREG AND ROCHÉ DRY 11. A FIRM FAVOURITE, ESPECIALLY WITH TIFF'S PIT-BULL CROSS 12. PLASTIC CUTLERY FROM @HOME 13. THE FIRST ART PIECE SIMON EVER BOUGHT, BY TREVOR PAUL 14. TIFF'S SHONGWENI FARMERS MARKET HAT 15. THEIR GARDEN LANDSCAPED BY CLINTON POTGIETER 16. A CLOSE UP OF THEIR "BARNEY" COUCH. *For captions relevant to other pictures in this chapter, please refer to the Addendum.*

SWEET POTATO, AUBERGINE & BEETROOT CRISPS

If you have a mandoline (the chips need to be cut thin) and a chip fryer, then you'll really enjoy making these. The red onion and yoghurt dip is also a winner. My vote for the tastiest chip definitely goes to our friend, Mr Sweet Potato… the low water content makes them crisp up like, well, crisps.

500g sweet potato (2 large ones)
• 300g beetroot (2 large ones)
• 350g aubergine (1 medium-sized one)
• vegetable oil for cooking

Slice the sweet potato, beetroot and the aubergine into 1mm thick pieces using a mandoline or electric meat slicer. Heat vegetable oil, preferably in a chip fryer, and when smoking hot, cook the veggie chips separately in batches. Cover the base of the chip fryer's basket with the veggie chips, one layer at a time. Then, drop into the oil. This ensures that the chips cook for the same amount of time. Shake the chip basket often to stop the chips from sticking together. Drain well on newspaper and gently salt while they are hot, so the salt sticks.

for the dip:
2 small red onions, shaved ultra thin
• 1 garlic clove, crushed • 400g thick
Greek-style yoghurt • 1t salt

This red onion dip is really a revelation… so easy to make and extremely tasty. Once you have finely sliced your red onions, rinse them in ice-cold water and dry well with a tea towel. Mix in with the garlic, yoghurt and salt and keep in the fridge before serving.

PS: If your crisps start going soft, place them on a baking tray and heat them gently to crisp them up. Serve with the yoghurt dipper. Awesome!

SERVES 4

 THE ITALIANS CALL AUBERGINE "MELANZANE", WHICH MEANS "CRAZY APPLE".

HEDGEHOG LOAF

Apart from his fascination with charcuterie (the craft of curing meat), Simon is a master baker… and, as with anything he does, he goes in for the kill.

2pkts (20g) instant yeast • 4 cups (1L) tepid carbonated water • 350g white bread flour • 700g brown bread flour • 3t white sugar • 2t salt • flour to cover the baking tray base

In a large mixing bowl, place 2 packets (20g) yeast and 2 cups (500ml) of tepid carbonated water. Leave this mixture to stand for about 20 minutes until it becomes a foamy mass. Weigh out the white and brown bread flour separately. Add the white bread flour into the yeast and water mixture, stirring in gradually to avoid lumps. The consistency should be like a thick cream. Leave covered with a dish towel for about an hour in a warm part of the kitchen. (Tip: if it's cold, ½ fill a sink with warm water and rest the bowl in that.)

After about 1 hour, the foamy dough should have at least doubled in size. Add 1½ cups (375ml) of tepid carbonated water then start adding the brown bread flour slowly. Mix with a wooden spoon, then by hand in the bowl, until a ball is formed. More water might need to be added to get the soft, spongy dough required. Knead for about 8 minutes. The consistency required is not sticky but not too firm.

Allow the bread dough to stand for 1 hour, covered with a dish towel. Once the dough has risen to double the size, knock it back and form a large round disk about 4cm thick. With a very sharp knife, cut cross-patterns 2cm deep and 4cm apart into the top of the loaf to make the pattern of a hedgehog's back. Cover the bread with a dusting of white bread flour and leave to rest for 20 minutes. Prepare your oven to 200℃ with the shelf in the middle.

For better crust and cooking, mist water into the oven at the start of baking. Bottles with triggers work the best and can be bought at most supermarkets. When the dough is initially placed in the oven, quickly spray fine mist into the oven - NOT onto the bread directly - before closing the door; repeat after 3 minutes. On the final spray, direct water onto the oven's floor. Remove the bread after 30 minutes. Leave to stand for a short while, then tuck in…

L-R: 1. SERIES OF LIGHT BOXES BY COLWYN THOMAS 2. TIFF'S SHOE CLOSET CONTAINING OVER 150 PAIRS 3. TIFF SAYS YOU CAN NEVER HAVE TOO MANY ORCHIDS… OR SHOES! 4. INDIGENOUS ALOES THRIVING IN THEIR 5-ACRE GARDEN 5. COLLECTION OF CRYSTAL FROM FRIENDS 6. TOWEL HOOK THAT GIVES NEW MEANING TO THE PHRASE, "GIVE IT HORNS!" *OPPOSITE:* ARTWORK BY TREVOR PAUL

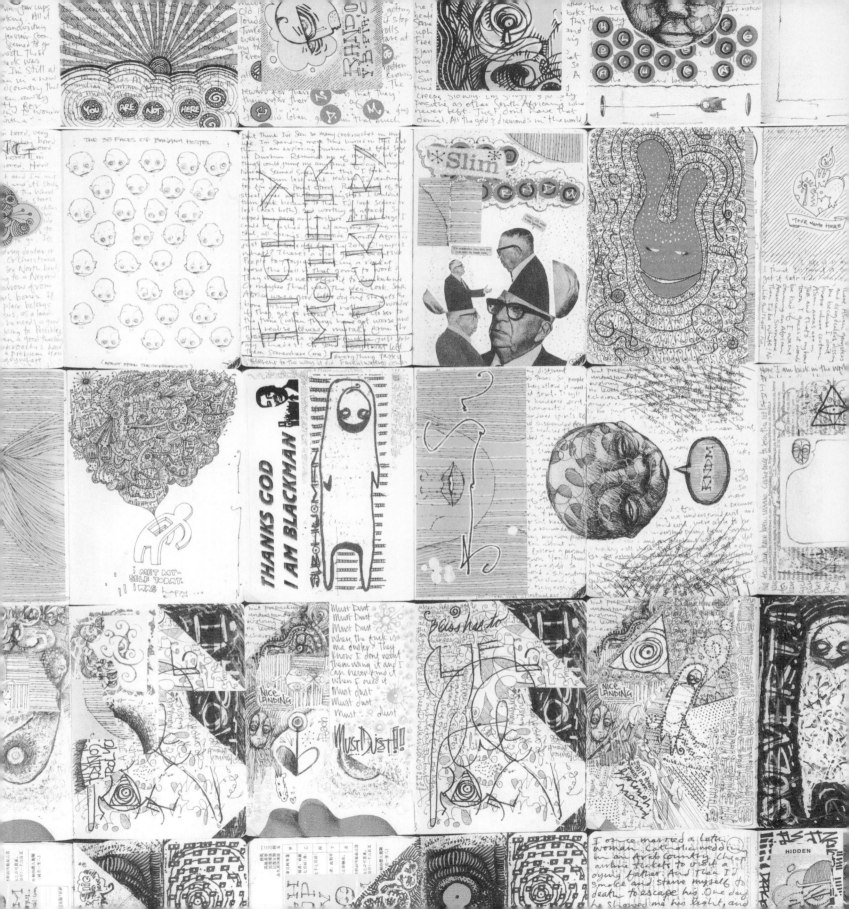

HALF & HALF RYE & WHOLEWHEAT BREAD

With wheat allergies abounding, rye bread has not only become popular, but an essential part of people's diet. But let's forget its goodness and celebrate its greatness…

2pkts (20g) dried yeast • 3t sugar • 3 cups (625ml) tepid water • 220g rye flour • 850g brown bread flour • 3t salt • 230g wholewheat flour • flour for dusting

Add 2 packets (20g) dried yeast and sugar to 1 cup (250ml) of tepid water and leave for 20 minutes. The yeast will foam up 4-5 times the original volume. Add all the rye flour into the yeast mixture, along with a further cup (250ml) of tepid water. You will be left with wet slurry. Leave for 1½ hours to rise.

The mixture should rise 2 to 3 times the volume after 1½ hours. Add half the brown flour and 1 cup (250ml) of tepid water and blend together. In a separate bowl, mix the remaining brown flour and the salt and add to the dough. Leave this for 1 hour. The texture should still be wet at this stage. Leave for a further hour before adding 230g wholewheat flour. The dough will become a dry ball that you need to knead for 8-10 minutes. Leave in the bowl, covered by a damp dish towel for 1½ hours.

Remove the dough from the bowl, knock back and form a disk about 5cm thick. Cut a 1cm cross through the top and place on a baking tray that has been liberally dusted with flour. Leave to stand for a further 30 minutes. At this stage the oven needs to be switched on and preheated to 200°C. Bake for 30 minutes. Remove and allow to cool for a bit, then tuck in…

 FLOUR WATER MIXTURE IS VERY SELDOM IDENTICAL, AS THE MOISTURE CONTENT IN THE FLOUR CHANGES DEPENDING ON WHERE YOU LIVE, HOW LONG THE PACKET HAS BEEN OPEN, ETC.

BOILED LEG OF LAMB

Roasting lamb was the only way I knew… until I had Sunday lunch at Simon and Tiff's home. I thought to boil lamb was sacrilege, but it's actually an old Welsh method (where plenty of lamb roam the hills). The meat remains perfectly moist and flavoursome and the caper sauce made with the lamb stock is the perfect accompaniment.

1½kg leg of lamb • 500g chicken wings • 2 bay leaves • 2t salt • 2t ground pepper • 750g baby carrots, cleaned • 750g baby potatoes, cleaned with skin on • 750g baby onions, peeled

Add the leg of lamb and chicken wings to a large pot and cover with cold water. Add the bay leaves, salt and pepper and cover. Bring to the boil and simmer for 2 hours (the chicken wings will add flavour to the stock). Clean and prepare the vegetables, then add to the stock after 2 hours have passed. Cook for a further 30 minutes at a gentle boil.

When the veggies are ready, remove the lamb onto a chopping board and the veggies into serving bowls. The meat should fall off the bone. As for the chicken wings, surprise your dogs with a tasty treat!

for the sauce:
20g butter • 20g flour • 300ml stock from pot • 3T capers, chopped finely and lightly rinsed • juice of ½ a lemon • salt & pepper to taste

Add the butter to a saucepan and heat until it foams. Add the flour to the pan and stir. Don't let the mixture catch. Add stock, from the pot on the stove, into the flour and butter mixture little by little to make a sauce. The sauce must not be too thick – it should be pouring cream in appearance. Add the chopped capers and the lemon juice. Cook over a low heat for 5 minutes and taste. Season at this point with salt, pepper and more lemon. Serve in large soup bowls, cover with stock and drizzle the caper sauce over the top.

SERVES 4

BOUILLA-BAISSE

Purists would start wailing at the very cheek of it. Calling this soup a bouillabaisse when you are not in Marseille, the home of the original, where the Rascasse (Scorpionfish) is the common local ingredient. So, whatever! It's a great, big exotic fish soup and the flavour of all the ingredients makes it one large party on a plate…

2-3kg firm fish meat plus heads & trimmings - mix fish type for flavour & colour. Use some small whole fish like reds (if available)
- **3 lengths celery • 2 bay leaves**
- **1 large fennel bulb, sliced finely**
- **8 cups (2L) cold water • 10 big tiger prawns**
- **1 portion (about 1½kg) frozen crab**
- **3 medium or 2 large onions, chopped coarsely**
- **2 carrots, chopped coarsely**
- **3 tots (75ml) Ricard • 2 tins (820g) tomatoes, chopped and drained • 20 frozen saldanha mussels in ½ shells (fresh is best so if you are near the beach, go pick some)**

Firstly, make fish stock with the heads and trimmings plus celery, bay leaves and fennel stalks and leaves. Add 2L of cold water. Then add the ingredients to a large pot, heat and boil gently with the lid off for about 40 minutes. Strain through a fine sieve and keep aside.

This meal is best cooked in a large paella pan. Add a small amount of oil to the pan, heat and add the prawns and crab. Heat until coloured pink, remove and keep to one side. Fry the onion, carrots and fennel bulb until the fennel and the onion start to colour. Add the fish portions. Shake around in the mixture for 3-4 minutes at high heat. Add the prawns and crab then flambé with 3 tots of Ricard.

Reduce heat to about half strength, ladle in 3-4 good ladlefuls of the fish stock and drained tomatoes. Cover with foil and leave to simmer for 10-12 minutes. After 10 minutes, remove the foil cover or lid and check the progress on the fish. You may need a little more stock. Now add the mussels and simmer for a further 10 minutes. Serve straight from the pan.

FOR SERVING: 3T parsley, chopped • 1 French loaf • *aioli

While the fish is cooking, make the aioli and slice the French loaf into rounds of about 2cm thick to make croutons. Dish the fish into large bowls, cover with broth and add the parsley and croutons.

SERVES 4-6

*FOR THE AIOLI RECIPE, PLEASE REFER TO THE ADDENDUM

AUTHENTIC MOUSSAKA

The authentic part of this dish is actually just being silly. I think Moussaka can only be authentic if eaten at the place of origin… like in a Greek taverna in the shadows of the Acropolis. There are so many versions but this one is delicious - cooked in individual aubergine halves, with fried potato, interleaved with a meat sauce made from red wine and cinnamon sticks. It's all topped with a fluffy béchamel that soufflés as it cooks due to the eggs that you've beaten in at the end. Oopa! Oopa!

for the meat sauce:
1 large onion, chopped finely • ¼ cup (60ml) olive oil • 4 garlic cloves, chopped roughly • 600g extra lean minced beef • 140g tinned tomato paste • 1 cup (250ml) red wine • 2 cinnamon sticks • 1t dried oregano • 2 bay leaves • 1 cup (250ml) water • 3 large potatoes, cut into 1cm slices with skin on

Fry the onions in the olive oil until translucent. Add the garlic and the meat and brown, separating the meat so it does not clump. Now add the tomato paste, red wine, cinnamon, dried oregano, bay leaves and water and stir. Put a lid on the pot and let this mixture simmer for 20-25 minutes. Meanwhile, deep fry the potato slices until light brown and tender. Drain on kitchen towel and set aside.

for the béchamel:
100g butter • ½ cup (125ml) flour • 50ml full cream milk • 1t salt • 1t white pepper • 1t freshly grated nutmeg • 2 large eggs • 3 large aubergines

Melt the butter until foaming and whisk in the flour. Allow this roux to cook for a couple of minutes until light brown. Now add the milk a little at a time, ensuring that you keep stirring and work each splash of milk into the flour mixture. Eventually a thick sauce will develop. Season with salt, pepper and nutmeg and remove from the heat. Crack the eggs into the mixture and whisk, then set aside.

SERVES 4

FOR THE REST OF THIS RECIPE, PLEASE REFER TO THE ADDENDUM

KEBAB MEATBALLS

It seems every country in the world has its own version of meatballs. We're big fans of the spicy stuff though, so a little Indian influence rounds off our version nicely. Adding the sweet potato is an interesting angle on the usual recipe, but try it, it's delish.

for the meatballs:
250g sweet potatoes • 500g lean mince • 1 egg • 1T garam masala • 1t salt

Boil the potatoes for approximately 20 minutes, start with cold water and bring to the boil. Plunge into cold water when cooked and allow to cool in a colander while you prepare the sauce. When the potatoes are cool, peel and mash finely. A potato ricer is the best, but the old fashioned way will do – just get in there with a fork once the initial mashing has been done. ADD NO LIQUID TO THE POTATO.

Blend the mince, egg, garam masala and potato into a bowl; add a pinch or 2 of salt and mix well. Leave to rest for 30 minutes in the fridge.

for the sauce:
1 medium onion, chopped finely • 1T canola or vegetable oil • 2 garlic cloves, chopped finely • 1 small chilli, chopped finely • 1T dhania powder • ½T cumin powder • 1T garam masala • ½t chilli powder • 1 tin Italian tomatoes, whole or chopped • 600ml water • 100ml yoghurt for serving

Fry the onion lightly in 1T canola or vegetable oil until translucent, not browned. Add the finely chopped garlic and chilli. Cook for about 5 minutes on a low heat. Add the spices, turn up the heat to medium, then stir continuously for 2 minutes before adding the tomatoes and reducing the heat. Add 600ml water and simmer very gently with the lid on for 30 minutes to let the flavour develop. Roll the mince into balls, the size of squash balls, and drop into the tomato sauce. Cook on a medium low heat for 25 minutes. You should get about 14-15 balls. Check seasoning, adjust to suit your palate and cook with the lid off for a further 15 minutes. Serve with roti or brown rice and a fresh mango, tomato, chilli salsa and the yoghurt.

SERVES 4

CHILLI CRAB

When crabs are up for grabs, there's only one way to do them justice… let them go out in a blaze of spicy glory. The Thai influence in this dish complements the subtly sweet crabmeat perfectly. Use as much chilli as you like, but be careful not to overpower the crab completely. Go on then… get cracking!

2 medium onions • 4T fish sauce • 6 red chillies, sliced coarsely (deseed if you don't like things too hot) • 5 large garlic cloves, sliced finely • 5 slices pickled ginger, chopped • 5cm ginger, julienned • 2kg crab • 100ml sweet Thai chilli sauce • 1 tin chopped tomatoes with juice • 300ml chicken stock 1 bunch coriander for garnish, chopped coarsley

Roughly chop the onions and fry for about half a minute. Then add 4T fish sauce, chilli, garlic and pickled ginger (which have been crushed in a pestle and mortar), followed by the julienned ginger. Stir so as not to burn the garlic. Add the crab and stir-fry until pink. Remove the crab and set aside. When the onions have softened, add the sweet chilli sauce and tinned tomatoes and cook for 5 minutes, stirring occasionally. Add the crab and chicken stock back into the pot. Stir and coat the crab every now and again - cook for about 35 minutes on a gentle heat. Top with coriander and serve with a small portion of basmati rice or some fresh bread to mop up the sauce.

SERVES 4

 CRABS HAVE VERY SMALL HAIRS ON THEIR CLAWS AND OTHER PARTS OF THEIR BODIES TO HELP DETECT WATER CURRENTS AND VIBRATIONS.

ORANGE CHIFFON CUPCAKES
with granadilla frosting

Everybody loves cupcakes, especially when they are so easy to make. Even Tiffany, who is probably the worst cook in the world (she will not dispute this, honestly), can make these. The icing is made with fresh granadilla pulp and then even more fresh pulp is spooned on after the icing has set. Well done, Tiff. Excellent cupcakes, cupcake! (I guess they are called Chiffon because they are light and fluffy?)

3 large eggs, separated • 110g sifted cake flour • 150g super-fine sugar • ½T baking powder • salt to taste • ¼ cup (60ml) vegetable oil • 90ml orange juice (freshly squeezed) • 1T orange zest • ½t vanilla extract

Separate the eggs and store at room temperature. In a mixing bowl, add the flour, 120g sugar, baking powder, salt and beat until combined. Then add the egg yolks, oil, orange juice, zest and vanilla extract, beating the ingredients until smooth. In a new bowl, beat the egg whites until foamy. Add 30g sugar and continue to beat. Add this mixture to the batter.

Transfer into cupcake rounds, bake at 170°C for 22-25 minutes. Pierce one with a toothpick and if it comes out clean, they are ready.

for the frosting:
1 large granadilla • 1½ cups (375ml) icing sugar

Scoop out the pulp from one large, ripe granadilla and mix with 1½ cups (375ml) icing sugar. Add a little more icing sugar if too watery. Once the cupcakes have cooled on a cooling wire, top each of them with 2t frosting. Once set, scoop a little more fresh granadilla pulp on top.

MAKES 12

"HORSE RIDING IN A LITTLE BLACK NUMBER? WHY NOT?" - TIFF

STUFF ABOUT SI...

YEARS OF 'WEAR & TEAR'? 45 **YOU LOVE?** Cooking **YOU HATE?** Violence and stupidity **SMELLS THAT RING YOUR BELL?** Bread and rain **FAVE PLACE IN SA?** Karoo & Northern KZN Coast **FAVE PLACE IN THE WORLD?** Home **WHAT ARE YOUR HOBBIES & PASSIONS?** Food and friends **IF "HOME" WAS A FOOD?** Bread **IS THIS YOUR DREAM HOME?** Almost... it's nearly done **WHAT WOULD YOU SERVE A GUEST IN OUR COUNTRY?** Lamb stew or cutlets, depending on the time of year **GUILTIEST PLEASURE?** Good whisky **WHAT SINGLE THING ABOUT YOUR HOME REFLECTS YOUR INDIVIDUALISM MOST?** No curtains **WHAT'S ONE WORD YOU WOULD USE TO SUM UP YOUR LIFE?** 45freakinyearsold!

STUFF ABOUT TIFF...

AKA? Tiffy, Tiff, Luvey, Stiffy, Stiffmeister, Stephania... and the one my husband and father use, "BEECH"! **EMOTIONAL AGE?** 22 **WHEN YOU'RE NOT WORKING?** I love riding my horse and being taken into fairy gardens with my niece and goddaughter. I am passionate about those things **DO YOU BRING YOUR PASSIONS HOME?** Absolutely, I love going to the stables on Saturday and Sunday and riding in the beautiful sunshine for a few hours... it touches my soul, and that makes me appreciate the insane horsey surroundings I live in. My niece, godchildren and nephews make me feel like the world is just fabulous, they LOVE our home and garden **WHAT MAKES YOUR NOSTRILS TINGLE?** Ooh, I love the smell of great food, there's such anticipation when people prepare good food **HOW DO YOU REALLY, REALLY SPOIL YOURSELF?** I love spa treatments, they are the ultimate luxury **EVER BROKEN INTO YOUR OWN HOME?** The last one, I thought I was Spiderman and fell off the window... hell, you were there **WHAT'S ONE WORD YOU WOULD USE TO SUM UP YOUR LIFE?** UNFUCKINBELIEVABLE!

FAVOURITE FOOD QUOTE?

there is one thing more exasperating than a wife who can cook and won't, and that's a wife who can't cook and will.
- ROBERT FROST

it was kind of boring for me to have to eat. I would know that I had to, and I would.

KATE MOSS

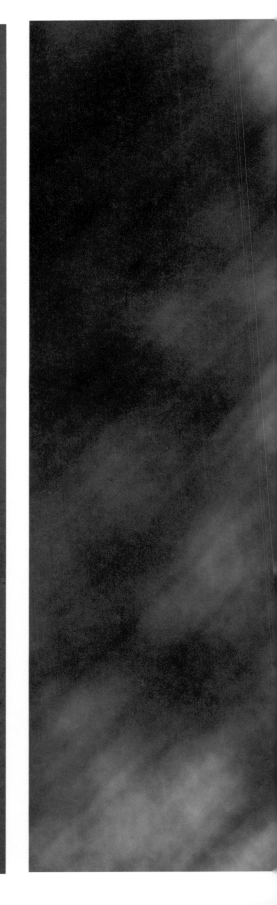

MENU
tarte tatin (caramelised apple tart)
tarte aux prunes et aux amandes (plum & almond tart)
meringues
parfait aux fraises (strawberry parfait)
far breton cake
crêpes au Cointreau (Cointreau pancakes)
marquise au chocolat

OBSERVATORY CAPE TOWN

Lucie Sue AND Tom

THE THING THAT STRUCK ME ABOUT MY NEW MATE, SUE DE MOYENCOURT, IS THE WARMTH SHE EXUDES (I JUST LOVE A GAL WHO OFFERS YOU A GLASS OF WINE WITHIN 5 MINUTES OF YOU ENTERING HER HOME).

Nowadays Sue is a ballet teacher… but she used to model for Dior and Courrèges in Paris in the 80's, was married to a French antique dealer, Gilles, who now operates out of the Albert Hall (subsequently their home is filled to the brim with tons of interesting and priceless antiques), and she lived and danced in Paris for years. With such an alluring past it's no wonder she came across as such a shiny and happy person. After a subsequent night out with her at the *Alliance Française* watching unplugged music, my suspicions were confirmed… she was unashamedly shiny… and really nice too!

If there's one thing that all mothers can't hide, it's the love they have for their children, and this is no more obvious than when Sue is with her kids, Tom and Lucie. Tom (24) is a great golfer, studied Business Science Finance, has got a very preppy French style with a touch of rockabilly, and looks about 15… unfair really. His sis, Lucie (26), is one of the most creative architecture students in her year at UCT, occupies the best room in the house (the attic), has been making homemade pasta since she was 10, makes crockery for her father with amusing French sayings on them (they are a more innocent version of Hylton Nel) and has made props, like mud banners with "Welcome Miss Amelia Earhart" sewn on in cowries and cool looking Voodoo dolls, for Mira Nair's movies. Needless to say, Sue has two very multi-talented children. Sue's home is known as the dessert capital of Cape Town (her desserts are very French in style and flavour), "I always think there's something special about puddings. When you bring them out - even if the rest of the meal has been a disaster - everyone says, 'Oh how lovely!" Which is exactly like Sue, "How lovely".

1. THE HEAD OF THE HOUSE, SUE 2. EVERYBODY LOVES PARFAIT! 3. THE FAMILY'S PET, MIU-MIU. GET IT?! 4. LUCIE'S HANDCRAFTED BOWL 5. FAR BRETON CAKE 6. SCULPTURE BY MOSES MANGAISO 7. MADEMOISELLE LUCIE IN HER STUDIO 8. AN OLD PARISIAN WEDDING PRESENT 9. TOM ON THE MOVE 10. BUBBLY WITH A TWIST 11. VIEW OF THE FAMILY HOME FROM THEIR FYNBOS GARDEN 12. SUE'S WELL-UTILISED KITCHEN 13. GILLES HAS A GREAT EYE! 14. LUCIE POSING FOR HER SELF-PORTRAIT 15. ENTRANCE MIRROR MADE OF CARVED BONE 16. OLD FRENCH ASHTRAY. *For captions relevant to other pictures in this chapter, please refer to the Addendum.*

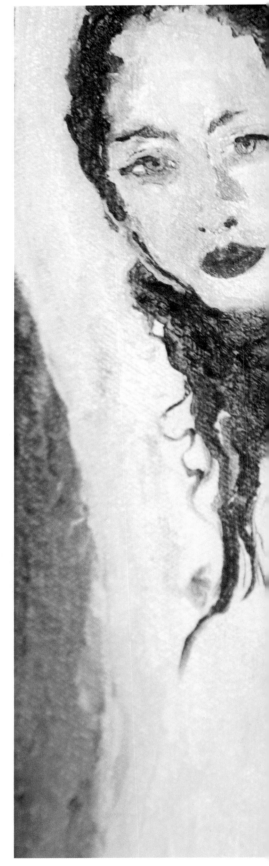

TARTE TARTIN

(caramelised apple tart)

When friends invite Sue away on weekends, it's usually on condition she brings one of these. This is Bocuse's version, a prominent nouvelle cuisine chef considered to be one of the finest chefs of the 20th century.

**125g butter • 100g sugar
• 1kg Granny Smith apples**

Generously grease the base of a non-stick tart tin or ovenproof dish, with 100g butter. Sprinkle over 50g sugar. Peel the apples, cut them into quarters and arrange them in the dish, squashing them tightly together. Sprinkle over the rest of the sugar and pour over 25g melted butter. Place the dish on the hot stove for around 20 minutes. The sugar should caramelise but remain pale brown.

**for the pastry:
1 cup (250g) flour • 1 egg
• 200g butter, softened • rind from
1 medium-sized lemon**

Mix the flour, egg and softened butter into a soft pastry (it should be difficult to roll). To give the pastry a nice tang, add a little grated lemon peel. Cover the pan with this pastry, and push the edges in around the apples. Bake for half an hour in a preheated oven at 190℃. Turn it out onto a plate and serve lukewarm.

SERVES 8

TARTE TATIN WAS A HAPPY ACCIDENT THAT OCCURRED AT *HOTEL TATIN* IN FRANCE IN 1898. THE HOTEL'S COOK AND PART OWNER, STÉPHANIE TARTIN, LEFT THE APPLES COOKING FOR TOO LONG, SO TO RESCUE THE DISH SHE CREATED AN UPSIDE DOWN TART WHICH THE GUESTS LOVED!

Apple Tart. Fair Lady   oven 190°C   6 Golden Delicious
                                                   250 ml apple purée
250 g flour   2 tbls apricot jam
125 g butter   1 tbls water
2   tbls sugar
pinch salt

Place flour in bowl. Add butter, sugar + salt, work with finger
tips til flour + butter are blended. Add some drops water if
necessary. Shape in ball. Press dough with fingertips into
unbuttered 23 cm tart dish. Fill case with purée, sweetened to
taste. Arrange 3 pieces spirally. Sprinkle with 1 tbls sugar.
Slice apples thinly. Fill case with purée. Mix jam + water, boil till
bake at 190 for 30 min. Mix jam + water, boil till
is baked, spoon over hot jam mixture.

Cream fat + sugar. Gradua
in baking powder + sifted
o milk, egg to to
in chick in to

TARTE AUX PRUNES ET AUX AMANDES
(plum & almond tart)

Sue has experimented with all sorts of combinations on this basic pâté brisée (light, flaky pastry dough), and after many delicious trial and error attempts, this one has come out tops. The red beads in the picture are pomegranate seeds, just added for decorative purposes. A mixture with circles of peaches and plums tends to look prettier. This is a light dessert, and a tart, fruity end to the meal!

for the pastry:
250g flour • 125g butter • 1 egg
• 50g almonds, ground

Mix the ingredients (except the almonds) together quickly to form a uniform pastry and pat it into a ball. Keep in a cool place for 30 minutes… this helps it roll out more easily. Roll the pastry out flat before lining the bottom and sides of a large tart tin. Prick the base and sprinkle over 50g ground almonds.

for the filling:
1kg plums, halved • 50g flaked almonds • 5/6T sugar (to taste)

Wash the plums, slice them in 2, remove the pips, and lay them on the pastry and almond base. Throw over some flaked almonds and a liberal sprinkling of sugar, to taste. Bake the tart in a preheated oven at 200°C for 30 minutes. Turn out and allow to cool. As mentioned before, this is also delicious served with a mixture of peaches and plums.

SERVES 10-12

"NOW GO FOR A JOG. OR A CYCLE. SERIOUSLY."
- LUCY

MERINGUES

This is Sue's mother's recipe, good for using up the egg whites left over from the parfait or crème brûlée… if you've made one!

egg whites from 4 eggs • 120g sugar

Beat the egg whites until really stiff then gradually add in the sugar. Spoon into spiky piles on a silicone baking sheet. Bake for an hour between 150°C (if you like them a bit brown) and 120°C. Once baked to your liking, prise them off the sheet, turn them onto their sides, switch off the oven, close the oven door quickly and leave them to cool in the oven overnight. If you prefer your meringues less chewy, cook them for longer in the oven at a very low heat.

SERVES 4-6

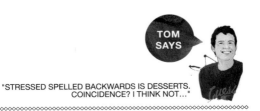

TOM SAYS

"STRESSED SPELLED BACKWARDS IS DESSERTS. COINCIDENCE? I THINK NOT…"

Dear Luce

thank u so much this extravagant it made a dept coffee-maker HAPPY! couldn't having some ar my drunken s paint you this card. lots of love,
Alice

MALIBU
CARIBBEAN
WHT RUM
WITH
COCONUT

THE LARGEST BURN
CANDLES

is working in a coffee shop at Notting
I'm working at 192 - a famous resta
ing hill 300m. from where we stay. I'm q
learned there I've done the training there a
dy as I could be for the opening in thing
ich I am quite Nervous after having read
in the stay about the place & all the famous
used hang out there

we're also the new locals at the Notti
Bar/Club that I'm certain you
& the MauMau Bar which is not as cool
but still pretty good - really trendy
very trendy peop!

live. this CRAZY Japanese guy tsu
ery wealthy Jap. family & who's been stu
all its forms for the last 17 years! He
the lifestyle I dream of. Her friends
and has been our "tourguide" since we arri

might also be working some weekends at the
his ultra traditional Pub - The Earl of Lons
te funny inside. the owners really cool alu
pints of Cider & making me try all these d
of which we like none but he's quite dete
ub is even closer than 192. I can see it from

L–R: 1. WHERE SUE UNWINDS AFTER TEACHING BALLET 2. A HANDMADE CARD FROM LUCIE'S BEST FRIEND 3. CANDLES ARE OFTEN USED TO LIGHT UP THE HOUSE 4. A PAGE FROM LUCIE'S WELL-DOCUMENTED DIARY 5. SUE'S R30 BARGAIN PICTURE FROM THE MILNERTON CAR BOOT SALE 6. BALLET COSTUME ACCESSORIES FOUND AROUND THE HOUSE OPPOSITE: A POSTER LUCIE BROUGHT BACK FROM BARCELONA

PARFAIT AUX FRAISES
(strawberry parfait)

Always a festive finish to a summer party, you can make this in a beautiful mould and pour a colourful coulis over it as you take it out. This can be made with peaches or granadillas, all of which are delicious too. According to Sue, this has evolved over the last 20 years from a torn-out magazine recipe. The family enjoys it every Christmas!

175g sugar • 3 egg yolks, beaten • 500g strawberries, stems removed & blended • 2 cups (500ml) cream

Place the sugar in a pot. Wet the sugar slightly and bring it to the boil. Beat the egg yolks in a bowl and pour the sugary syrup onto them in a thin drizzle while beating vigorously. Continue beating until the mixture is cold and takes on a mousse-like texture. Fold the strawberries into the cold mixture. Whip the cream, fold all the ingredients together and freeze. Remove from the freezer 1 hour before serving and place it in the fridge for the correct texture (must appear smooth rather than crystal-like). To finish, drizzle over with your choice of coulis and… voilà!

SERVES 12

PARFAIT IS A FRENCH WORD LITERALLY MEANING "PERFECT" THAT IN 1894 STARTED BEING USED WHEN REFERRING TO A TYPE OF FROZEN DESSERT.

FAR BRETON CAKE

Somewhat like a custard tart, without the pastry crust, Far Breton is a humble yet luscious, perfectly easy and nutritious cake for kids' lunch boxes, with morning coffee, at snacktimes or for a dessert. Traditionally you leave the pips in, but if you don't want to be liable for your friend's crown, get stoned (de-pipped) prunes! This recipe is adapted from the classic no-frills *Tante Marie* cookbook.

1 cup (250g) flour • 200g sugar • 4 eggs • 3 cups (750ml) milk • 37ml rum • 50g raisins • 12 prunes

In a bowl, mix the flour, sugar, eggs (one by one), milk and rum. Then add the raisins and prunes, which have been soaked overnight in some rum. Butter a large round cake tin, pour in the mixture and bake in a preheated oven for 1 hour at 180°C.

SERVES 8

SUE SAYS

"BEWARE OF PRUNE PIPS!!!"

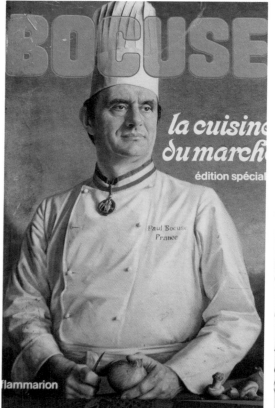

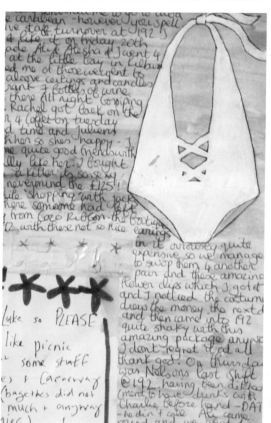

L–R: 1. THE GUEST ROOM UPSTAIRS 2. A COLLECTION OF FRENCH POETRY, PLAYS, AND OTHER FRENCH LITERATURE 3. THEIR "GREEK TAVERN" COURTYARD, USED MOSTLY IN SUMMER 4. SUE'S OLD RECIPE BOOK BY FAMOUS FRENCH CHEF, BOCUSE 5. LUCIE'S ARTISTIC RECORDINGS OF HER LONDON ADVENTURES 6. THE GUEST ROOM'S PATCHWORK QUILT

CRÊPES AUX COINTREAU
(Cointreau pancakes)

Sue had to steal her father's Cointreau for this, as it's a bit pricey, but you can substitute Grand Marnier, Van der Hum or Witblits. Big brownie points if you can flambé with flair…

for the crêpes:
1 cup (250g) flour • 2 cups (500ml) milk {or 1 cup (250ml) milk and 1 cup (250ml) water for lighter crêpes} • 3 eggs • 2T cooking oil

Place the flour in a bowl. Pour in 1 cup (250ml) milk, beating with an electric beater to make sure there are no lumps. Add the eggs one by one, then the oil and the rest of the liquid. Make the crêpes in a large flat crêpe pan and pile them on a plate, ready for the filling.

for the crême pâtissère filling:
4 egg yolks • 40g flour • ½ cup (125g) sugar • 2 cups (500ml) milk • 4T Cointreau (or more…)

Put the egg yolks, flour and sugar in a bowl and beat well, adding the milk. Then add 2T Cointreau. Pour into a saucepan on a moderate heat and keep stirring until the mixture thickens. Don't worry if it boils a bit. Spread some crème pâtissière onto each crêpe, roll the crêpes and line them up next to each other in a long oven dish. Just before serving, heat the dish, sprinkle over with 50g sugar, heat the remaining Cointreau, pour on, and flambé.

SERVES 4

MARQUISE AU CHOCOLAT

It's common knowledge that the French, particularly Parisian's, aren't the friendliest lot. So when you do come across a friendly, local face it's quite something. Framboise was one of those special few who immediately befriended and was kind to Sue when she first arrived in Paris as a "very naive South African". Sue told me this dessert is just a small taste of that kindness. This is honestly the ultimate chocolate iced dessert… you'll seduce anyone with this.

300g dark chocolate • 6t strong coffee • 150g butter • 4 eggs, separated into whites & yolks

Melt 300g dark chocolate with 6t strong coffee in a bain-marie (double boiler). Add 150g butter and melt together. Remove from the bain-marie and add 4 egg yolks into the chocolate mixture, beating vigorously. In a separate bowl, beat the egg whites until stiff. Fold the stiff egg whites carefully into the chocolate mixture, place in a loaf tin and freeze for at least 4 hours.

SERVES 8-10

HENRY STUBBE WAS A PHYSICIAN WHO CONSIDERED DRINKING CHOCOLATE ONCE OR TWICE A DAY AN EXCELLENT CURE FOR FATIGUE CAUSED BY HARD WORK.

SUE SAYS...

I LOVE... Paris in the springtime, laughing, my job, romantic gardens, swimming at Cape Infanta, Lucie and Tom (duuh!). I NEED... an unself-catered holiday and a handyman. I EAT... winegums. I TASTE... vegetables and herbs from my garden. I BELONG TO... the Mile High Club. I ENJOY... acting in TV commercials (the food is always so good on set) and combining outspoken people of all ages at dinner parties. I LISTEN TO... Schubert, Fasil Say. I'M READING... a biography of Flaubert. I LIKE WATCHING... (or rather perving over) the Cuban dancer Carlos Acosta on YouTube. I SPEND MOST DAYS... working or playing spider solitaire. I THINK FASHION IS... ridiculous (I did a stint in haute couture modelling in Paris). I BELIEVE SOUTH AFRICA IS... hard to beat.

LUCIE SAYS...

I LOVE... palm trees, red lipstick, Russia, rabbits, my grandparents, oil painting, the Salvation Army shops, Cape Infanta. I NEED... a large trust fund. I EAT... pasta, pasta, pasta! I TASTE... Tommy's sweet and sour pork fillet Asian taste-explosion-in-your-mouth dish. I wish he'd make it again! Apparently it took all day. I BELONG TO... a chilli sauce making club (the best birds-eye chillies come from Tatjana's grandmother's bush, which is in Durban somewhere). I ENJOY... dancing. I LISTEN TO... Tommy's DJ mixes (these always make you want to dance), Ella Joyce Buckley and Dear John love Emma, (both excellent and beautiful in their own ways). I'M READING... four books at once: the interminable but amazing *Anna Karenina*, *Bob Dylan Chronicles*, *Bury Me Standing* (a book about Romanian gypsies), and Jilly Cooper's *Polo* (for the 2nd time). I LIKE WATCHING...our cat Miu-Miu, she's a nut job. I SPEND MOST DAYS... slaving away at architecture school, scheming what it is I'm going to do when/if I ever get out of architecture school (probably not architecture but something chilled like jam-making or crocheting). I THINK FASHION IS... oxygen. I BELIEVE SOUTH AFRICA IS... going to enjoy a shiny and happy future!

TOM SAYS...

I LOVE... good waves, my turntables, hopping on a plane, espadrilles, red pants, beautiful smiles, the Xmas eve dancefloor action, golf. I NEED... to clean my room, ASAP, and to explore Madagascar. I EAT... French/Italian/Thai/Japanese. I TASTE... Lucie's sage chicken, I wish she'd make it more often, it's really quick and easy to make. I REMEMBER... parrot-fish with garlic on the braai in Mozam. It was legal back then, I think... I BELONG TO... the rat race. I ENJOY... *Anatoli, Mzoli's, Minato's, Fiction,* and *The Assembly*. I LISTEN TO... the Rolling Stones and everything else. I'M READING... Oscar Wilde - one day I'll (hopefully) be well-read. I LIKE WATCHING... my shares go up. I SPEND MOST DAYS... breathing and stuff. I THINK FASHION IS... random. I BELIEVE SOUTH AFRICA IS... where the heart is!

I love Thanksgiving turkey... it's the only time in Los Angeles that you see natural breasts.

ARNOLD SCHWARZENEGGER

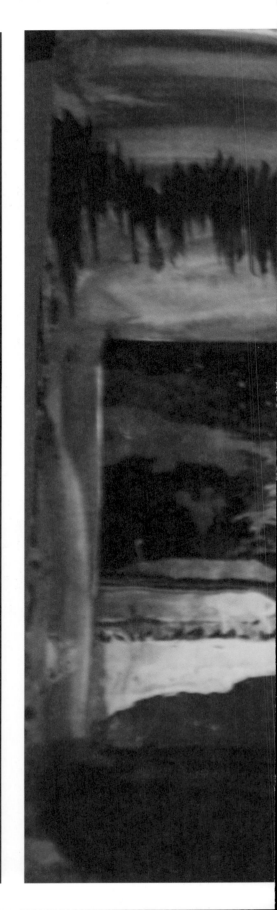

a nice King and has really co...
of stewardessing in the caribb...
that with the massive staff...
really feel old school & like...
September - Jacinta Jade Ali...
a really nice dinner at the...
the restaurant reminded me o...
in florence with the alcove a...
in wine bottles we drank 7...
between us and where there A...
like crazy as girls do. Rachel...
monday and I met her 4 (offee...
she had a really good time...
moved back in with her so...
think have become quite...
Ali. I really really like...
this costumes its a kille...
I had to get it nevermi...
I discored it while sho...
after a shift where som...
behind a bag from Ca...
across from TIZ with...

✷ ✷ ✷ ✷ ✷

✷ Hey Luce! ✷

Am at Gold with Luke so
come join me.
doesn't really look like pi
weather but bought some
anyway : tomatoes + (
bread (bagette
look up 2 much i
its healthier)
And Stunning WIN
white + coral Sand

MENU

hot cross buns
toasted English muffins with mascarpone & caramel
fig & honey yoghurt cups
banana buttermilk pancakes
flowering courgettes in a tempura batter
hollandaise sauce on a fillet steak sandwich
roast chicken with lemon, garlic & rosemary
stewed figs in red wine
chocolate cheesecake

Catherine

KLEINEFONTEIN
W. Cape

WHEN LAST DID YOU ENJOY THE RITUAL OF LIGHTING A CHANDELIER FULL OF CANDLES, INSTEAD OF FLICKING A SWITCH? OR BEING OUT OF CELL PHONE RANGE FOR DAYS ON END. KLEINEFONTEIN IS A CAPE DUTCH RETREAT SOME 4 HOURS FROM CAPE TOWN AND THE PLACE CATHERINE RAPHAELY HEADS TO AS OFTEN AS HER TIME ALLOWS.

As co-founder of Uncharted Africa Safari Co., life lived in the African wilderness is second nature to Catherine. Since the founding of the company in 1992, Catherine and her business partner, Ralph Bousfield, have set up a myriad of camps in remote areas of Botswana that access some of the most beautiful landscapes of the Makgadikgadi Pans. Their four camps (Jack's camp, San Camp, Camp Kalahari and Planet Baobab) have seen Catherine's natural style create environments ranging from luxurious 1920's luxury and style of a bygone era in Jack's Camp, to the affordable, out-of-this-world Planet Baobab. After 17 years based in Botswana, Catherine has returned to Cape Town to run operations from a South African base, but it's the need for those wide open African spaces that compels her to speed her off through Robertson and Worcester and down dusty roads that end at Kleinefontein, on the Duivenhoks river estuary.

The farmhouse kitchen is the centre of the Kleinefontein house. The gas stove boils the water that feeds early morning espressos, bakes cheesecakes and toasts crumpets. With its ever changing natural light, it's a little like being in a Dutch masterpiece painting, especially as the late afternoon sun casts sharp shafts of light across the house. Eventually the chandelier of candles is lit, the kitchen flickers alive and the cooking and the feasting begins…

1. HOW TO MAKE DIETERS GREEN WITH ENVY 2. THE HOME'S ENTIRE SOURCE OF LIGHT IN ONE TIN... CATHERINE'S MATCH CONTAINER 3. LINNWARE CROCKERY 4. IT WAS EASTER, SO THIS WAS THE PERFECT TREAT 5. CORAL COLLECTED FROM THE BEACH 6. THE SUNBIRDS' FAVOURITE FLOWERS 7. THE CUTLERY IS KEPT IN FORKIN' OLD TINS 8. A REPLICA VOORTREKKER SWING-BED IN CATHERINE'S FAVOURITE BEDROOM 9. THE SPRING WATER LILY POND THAT WE SWAM IN 10. NATIONAL MONUMENT PLAQUE ON THE HOUSE 11. CATHERINE'S HOUSE DATES BACK TO 1789 12. INTRICATE CROSS-STITCH BED COVER 13. CATHERINE HAPPY AND AT HOME IN HER KITCHEN 14. STINKWOOD WELSH DRESSER 15. THE SAND DUNES ALONG THE BEACH ARE CRAWLING WITH GIANT LAND SNAILS 16. DEITZ LANTERNS ARE HANDY IN A HOUSE WITH NO ELECTRICITY. *For captions relevant to other pictures in this chapter, please refer to the Addendum.*

HOT CROSS BUNS

It's the photographer's lovely wife, Camilla, who brings along the hot cross buns for a breakfast feast. Based on a family recipe with the addition of buttermilk and a sugary frosting, they are the perfect accompaniment to trays laden with cutlery, crockery, napkins, cafetières shrouded in cosies (to keep them piping hot), crumpets, muffins, mascarpone cheese and Argentinian caramel.

for the buns:
1½ cups (375ml) milk • 1½ cups (375ml) buttermilk • 1½ cups (375ml) sugar • ¾ cup (180ml) water • 200g butter • 3 eggs • 9 cups (1¼L) cake flour • 6t mixed spice • 2t salt • 1 cup (250ml) sultanas • 2 cups (500ml) raisins • zest of 2 oranges • zest of 1 lemon • 2pkts (20g) yeast

for the crosses:
1pkt Woolies puff pastry, defrosted but kept cold

for the glaze:
mix 1 cup (250ml) sugar with a little cold water to make a sugary paste

Heat the milk, buttermilk, water, sugar, zest and butter over medium-high heat until the butter has melted. Set aside to cool until lukewarm. Beat in the eggs. Sift the flour, mixed spice and salt into a bowl and add the sultanas and raisins. Sprinkle the yeast over the top. Add the milk mixture and mix until it comes together to form a dough. Leave to rise overnight. Knead on a floured surface until the dough is smooth. Divide into two and keep dividing each piece of dough until you have 36 pieces. Roll and shape each piece into a bun shape and place on a greased baking sheet. Roll out the pastry on a lightly floured surface and cut into strips - these are going to form the crosses. Brush the buns with water and lay the crosses over the buns tucking in the ends on the side of each bun. Preheat oven to 160°C, and mix together the ingredients for the glaze. Bake the buns for 15-20 minutes. Turn the oven up to 180°C. Remove the buns and brush with the sugary glaze and return to oven for a further 5-10 minutes until the crust is hard and sugary. These are perfect to freeze and defrost and will keep for 2 months.

MAKES 3 DOZEN

TOASTED ENGLISH MUFFINS

with mascarpone & caramel

Catherine happily admits that this isn't really a recipe, but an idea (of which she has many). It's her special KF (Kleinefontein) breakfast, "I got so many people into it and they'd never thought of it before... so simple, but so good. Perhaps because you have to burn it on the gas top toaster, so it's got that charcoal flavour!" Catherine normally serves creamed honey with the mascarpone but the jar of caramel was delish.

for the dulche de leche: (Latin American caramel spread)

South America is fiery but so sweet too. This caramel spread is enjoyed throughout Argentina, Mexico, Peru, Chile, Bolivia and Colombia as a spread for bread, pastries, cakes, crêpes and cookies. And in South Africa... for muffins.

4 cups (1L) milk • 1¼ cups (375ml) sugar • 1t vanilla • ¼t baking soda

Add all the ingredients to a heavy-bottomed saucepan and stir well to dissolve the sugar completely. Set the saucepan over medium heat and bring to the boil. Reduce to a very low heat and simmer for about 1-1½ hours, stirring frequently, until thickened and caramelised. Transfer to a clean glass jar and refrigerate. Will keep for 1-2 weeks.

Like I said, this isn't really a recipe, so just toast your muffin and get stuck in. Be generous with the mascarpone and caramel... we were!

MAKES ABOUT 3 CUPS

ORIGINALLY MADE FOR THE "DOWNSTAIRS" SERVANTS IN VICTORIAN SOCIETY, THE ENGLISH MUFFIN WAS MADE BY THE FAMILY BAKER FROM LEFTOVER DOUGH AND MASH. BUT ONCE THE "UPSTAIRS" FAMILY TASTED THESE TREATS, THEY DEMANDED TO HAVE THEM FOR THEMSELVES - ESPECIALLY FOR TEATIME.

L-R: 1. KUDU HORN TROPHY FROM WHEN THE HOUSE WAS USED AS A HUNTING LODGE BY THE MAYOR OF SWELLENDAM 2. GLORIOUS OLD VICTORIAN BATH 3. ANY BABOON CAN MAKE THIS EASY BREAKFAST SNACK 4. CATHERINE AGREES THAT FRESH IS ALWAYS BEST! 5. TEATIME! (ANY EXCUSE FOR SHORT BREAD BISCUITS) 6. THE LUNCH SPREAD *OPPOSITE:* ON A SCALE OF 1-10... THESE ARE 20!

FIG & HONEY YOGHURT CUPS

Sometimes in life, it's the simplest of meals that are the most memorable. To quote Alexis Soyer, a 19th century French chef, "It matters not how simple the food – a chop, steak or a plain boiled or roast joint, but let it be of good quality and properly cooked, and everyone who partakes of it will enjoy it." So the black figs were ripe and sexy, the yoghurt thick (double cream Greek), the pistachios organic and freshly toasted and the honey… badger friendly and very runny. This little sustenance builder was Catherine's friend, Byron's idea of a quick breakfast before a dip in the Duivenhoks River. Upon our return, refreshed and invigorated, it was time to make the real breakfast pancakes, which actually became lunch, and so the day rolled on…

fresh figs • honey • thick Greek yoghurt

Listen up: You can be fancy and call this a breakfast parfait, if you wish, and layer the fruit, nuts and yoghurt in between layers of toasted granola, or substitute sliced banana and caramel in between layers of yoghurt or even… well, the list is endless…

"I'M NOT A CHEF... I'M A SHOPPER..."
- CATHERINE

BANANA BUTTERMILK PANCAKES

for the pancakes:
1½ cups (375ml) cake flour • 2T sugar • 1T baking powder • 1t salt • 1 cup (250ml) buttermilk • ½ cup (125ml) full cream milk • 2 eggs • 2 bananas, mashed and added to the mix • 2T melted butter

Mix the cake flour, sugar, baking powder and salt together in a bowl. Beat together with the buttermilk, full cream milk and eggs. Then add the bananas and melted butter. Allow the whole lot to rest for about 15 minutes. Heat a frying pan to a medium-high heat and get flipping! Use 2T to make your pancakes, so they're a good size!

for serving:
seasonal fruit salad • mascarpone cheese • 200g streaky bacon, cooked • maple syrup

Serve the heap of pancakes with a fresh seasonal fruit salad (we used gooseberries, raspberries, mango and pomegranate seeds), mascarpone cheese, with crispy bacon and maple syrup on the side. Flippin' hell! Pancake heaven!

MAKES 12-14

THE LARGEST NUMBER OF PANCAKES TOSSED IN THE SHORTEST AMOUNT OF TIME IN THE UK IS 349 TOSSES IN 2 MINUTES. WE WEREN'T IN SUCH A RUSH…

FLOWERING COURGETTES

in a tempura batter

A visit to the Neighbourgoods Market in Salt River, Cape Town, is essential before heading off for a weekend away. You never know what's in season and what's going to catch your eye. Like the flowering courgettes I snapped up, and the buffalo mozzarella from South Africa's first herd of buffalo imported from Australia. Catherine took one look at the flowering zucchini and said, "stuff them with mozzarella and anchovies and deep fry them in a light batter", which we did.

for the tempura batter:
1 cup (250ml) flour • 200ml soda water • ½t salt • 8 courgettes/zucchinis with flower attached • 1 ball fresh buffalo mozzarella • 8 anchovies, drained of oil

Add 4T olive oil to a pan and fry the zucchinis gently on both sides until golden-brown. Drain on a kitchen towel and serve with lemon juice, salt and black pepper… or with store-bought pesto if you prefer.

SERVES 6

ALL THE FLOWERS ARE EATEN?

"COURGETTE" IS THE FRENCH FOR THE ITALIAN "ZUCCHINI". THE FLOWERS STILL ATTACHED ARE A SIGN OF A REALLY FRESH AND IMMATURE FRUIT. THEY'RE YUMMY TOO…

HOLLANDAISE SAUCE

on a fillet steak sandwich

Hollandaise sauce is one of the 5 sauces in the French haute cuisine "Mother Sauce" range. And "Oooh, La, La!", it's so delicious and easy to prepare. It's versatile too… not only is it a key ingredient in Eggs Benedict, it's also amazing with asparagus, potatoes and yes, of course, good red meat. Try it with a nice rare fillet, exactly as we did.

3 egg yolks • juice of 1 lemon • 1 cup (250ml) melted hot butter • salt & pepper to taste

Blend the egg yolks and lemon juice in an electric blender or with a hand-held blender, gradually pouring in the very hot, melted butter. Blend until thick and creamy and season with salt and pepper. Take a little care… it should be served warm, not hot! Over or under heating will make the sauce split, or separate. Then you'll have to split the kitchen… fast!

A MOTHER HEN TURNS HER EGG APPROXIMATELY 50 TIMES IN A DAY SO THE YOLK DOES NOT STICK TO THE SHELL.

ROAST CHICKEN

with lemon, garlic & rosemary

for the chicken:
10 potatoes, peeled and cut in half lengthways • 2 free-range chickens (about 1kg each) • 2 lemons, quartered • 3 whole lemons • 4 large sprigs of rosemary, trimmed of the leaves • 8 giant garlic cloves, chopped finely • another head of giant (elephant) garlic, separated into cloves for roasting • salt & pepper to taste • 80ml olive oil

Preheat the oven to 180°C. Bring the peeled potatoes to the boil for 10 minutes. Drain and toss in some olive oil. Place the chickens side-by-side in a roaster. Insert 4 quarters of lemon into the cavities as well as a sprig of rosemary and loosely tie the legs up with string. Pour some olive oil and some lemon juice, 1 lemon for each chicken, over the chickens and sprinkle the chopped garlic and loads of chopped rosemary over too. (I never put salt on my roast chicken when it's roasting, because, a famous Chef, Jacques Pepin, once told me you should only salt meat after cooking as it draws out moisture.) Season the chickens with black pepper and drizzle the olive oil equally over the skin. Place the potatoes around the chickens, flat sides down, along with the remaining, used lemon quarters (remember to remove the lemons half an hour into the cooking process or they'll burn). Add the garlic cloves in their skins, just half an hour before the chicken is due to come out of the oven otherwise they'll also burn. Place the pan on the middle shelf of the oven at 180-200°C for 70-80 minutes. Baste with the pan juices halfway through cooking.

for the gravy:
To make a basic pan gravy, remove the chicken and potatoes to a serving dish and cover with foil. Add a little water if there is not much gravy, and squeeze in some more lemon juice from the remaining lemons. Season with salt and black pepper and put the roasting pan on top of the stove. Using the heat of two hot plates, loosen all the left over bits of garlic, rosemary and chicken skin with an egg lifter and make sure it's almost amalgamated into a tangy jus. Strain the gravy through a wire mesh into a gravy boat and only add a little flour and butter if you prefer a thicker consistency.

SERVES 6-8

FOR THE REST OF THIS RECIPE (AND SOME USEFUL TIPS), PLEASE REFER TO THE ADDENDUM.

STEWED FIGS IN RED WINE

250g (¼kg) dried figs • 1½ cups (375ml) red wine (we used Merlot) • 8 whole green cardamom pods • 1T runny honey • 8 fresh figs • mascarpone to serve

Add the dried figs, red wine, cardamom pods and honey to a pot and simmer over a low heat for an hour, stirring gently at random intervals. The figs should maintain their shape. Turn off the heat and let the figs rest in their juices for at least an hour. Serve lukewarm with a scoop of mascarpone and 2 fresh figs per serving. Slice a cross in the top of each fig and push with your fingers up from the base to open the figs up and to expose their beautiful ruby flesh.

SERVES 4-6

HONEYBEES AREN'T BORN KNOWING HOW TO MAKE HONEY... THE YOUNGER BEES ARE TAUGHT BY THE MORE EXPERIENCED ONES.

CHOCOLATE CHEESECAKE

for the crumb crust:
2 cups (500ml) Marie biscuits, finely crushed • 113g butter, melted • 1t cinnamon

Mix together the finely crushed Marie biscuits (only use one packet and don't crush it too finely if you prefer a bit of extra texture) with the melted butter and cinnamon (add the cinnamon until you can taste it quite strongly, if you like it spicy). Line the base and sides of a springform tin with the mix, taking care to ensure that the corners are not too thick. Do not butter the tin or it will get soggy, there's enough butter in the crust already. Put in the fridge to chill while you make the filling.

for the filling:
2½ bakkies (625ml) smooth cottage cheese • 1 bakkie (250ml) sour cream • 3 eggs • ¾ cup (180ml) sugar • 1t vanilla • 200g dark chocolate, melted (use only Cadbury's Bournville and not Nestle or Beacon) • 2T cocoa • 60g melted butter

Preheat oven to 175-180°C. Mix the cottage cheese and sour cream and blend well. Add the eggs, sugar and vanilla and beat well. Mix in the melted chocolate, cocoa and lastly melted butter. Beat until it's evenly distributed. Pour into crust and bake for 45 minutes.

When you take it out of the oven, it may appear unset. Leave it in the fridge and it will solidify. This cake tastes better if served the next day.

SERVES 12

THE PHENYETHYLENE AND ANANDAMIDE CONTAINED IN CHOCOLATE HAVE ANTI-DEPRESSANT PROPERTIES.

L-R: 1. PAINTING BY CATHERINE'S GRANDMOTHER 2. OLD VINES HANGING OVER THE STOEP 3. IT'S A TOUGH LIFE! 4. CATHERINE'S FRIEND, LUCIE'S DELICIOUS ROASTED SWEET POTATOES WITH WHOLE GARLIC & LEMON PEEL 5. AN AUTHENTIC SWING-BED FROM AN ORIGINAL VOORTREKKER WAGON 6. THE QUAINT NEARBY FISHING COTTAGE *OPPOSITE:* THERE'S NOTHING MORE REFRESHING THAN COOL, SPRING WATER

you can never have enough garlic. with enough garlic, you can eat *The New York Times.*

– MORLEY SAFER

Q&A WITH CATHERINE

MEALS YOU'D LOVE TO REWIND...
I used to have TV dinners in London with AA Gill and his girlfriend, Nicola Formby. All the TV stations used to send him tapes to review for his *Sunday Times* TV column. Once, Nicola made wild duck... Adrian singed off the feathers. The basting was made with port, marmalade and figs, it was delicious.

EXOTIC FOODS NOT WORTH THE TRIP...
The most exotic thing I have ever eaten was breaded sheep's testicles, which was ok, but not good enough. And crocodile, which is very oily. I actually have a pet crocodile called Levi back in Francistown.

COOKING YOU'LL ALWAYS LOVE...
My mom's cooking (or more like her staff's cooking)! They'd make lovely old-fashioned dishes like Chicken Gaston Gérard cooked in the electric frying pan with cream and Gruyére cheese and white wine and mustard.

THE FOOD'S FAR, THE MEMORIES CLOSE...
In Croatia on a holiday with my folks, my mom would go to the market everyday. She is a compulsive marketeer. I think I would be more of a foodie if I had the time and wasn't such a generalist.

YOUR SURVIVAL FOOD...
I lived in Francistown for 17 years, which has to be the most unglamorous and most unromantic place in the world. One solace was that it had a great Indian restaurant.

YOUR MOST DRAMATIC MEAL...
In Marrakech, I went to this fantastic restaurant where they would debone the lamb with huge swords in only a few minutes... it was food theatre.

YOUR TASTIEST TIDBIT ABOUT YOUR HOME...
Lord Charles Somerset was the Governor of the Cape from 1814 to 1826 and he is supposed to have used or owned my farm as a hunting box. During that time Dr James Barry was a medical official in the colonial British Government. Allegedly, Dr James Barry was actually a "she", (her real name, Miranda) who had to cross-dress as a man in order to overcome prevailing gender issues of that era. The juicy part of the story is that apparently, Dr Barry and Lord Charles used to have secret, romantic escapades at Kleinefontein. I love this story... I'm sure they weren't the first and they aren't the last... my home is an intensely romantic and conveniently remote location. People can't help but fall in love at Kleinefontein.

fish, to taste right, must swim three times - in water, in butter, and in wine.

POLISH PROVERB

MENU

limoncello
Parmesan custard with anchovy toast
ruote with boerewors & yellow pepper sauce
chicken fricasséed with rosemary & lemon juice
spaghettini with crayfish
strawberry ice-cream
cherry clafoutis
Swiss chard torta (spinach tart)

graeme

GLENASHLEY

I MET GRAEME MANY MOONS BACK WHEN HE WAS DOING A GUEST CHEF EVENING AT DURBAN'S ICONIC *BEAN BAG BOHEMIA* RESTAURANT. MY WIFE AND I WERE SEATED NEXT TO GRAEME'S PARTNER, THE ARTIST DERYCK HEALEY… THE EVENING LASTED WAY INTO THE EARLY HOURS OF THE MORNING AND THE FRIENDSHIP AND SHARING AROUND THE TABLE HAS CONTINUED EVER SINCE.

Graeme's home in Glenashley has a balcony with a view of the sea that makes cooking an even more pleasurable experience. But you'll find him in his second home in Essex when the sun is shining in the Northern Hemisphere. I have spent many a weekend in the English countryside, cooking, enjoying glorious summer evenings and listening to some of Graeme's very entertaining tales.

His interest in food was born out of necessity. "The first chicken I ever cooked, I left the plastic bag with the gizzards and neck inside. I knew then I had to do something about this and enrolled at *Cordon Bleu's* 3-month programme. It was 1976 and the school was fiercely strict. The mornings were spent preparing

a 3-course meal, which was then inspected (Nazi style) at 12. The afternoon demos included expensive ingredients… lobster mousse, grouse, and so on. After this demo, you could bid to take the dishes home. I always took them home for Deryck." Graeme could have continued for an additional 3 months at *Cordon Bleu*, but decided he really did not want to know how to prepare a buffet in aspic (savoury jelly made from meat stock).

Graeme's menu consists of unashamedly simple, easy and unpretentious cooking and I can vouch for every meal, as I have eaten them all on many occasions. Even if you think the chicken with rosemary and lemon is too easy for words, just try it… it's amazing how simple food is sooo good.

1. GRAEME'S LIFE IN HIS GLENASHLEY HOME IS A REAL BEACH 2. ART BY DERYCK HEALEY 3. TAMLYN MARTIN PAINTING IN THE KITCHEN 4. THERE'S ALWAYS TIME FOR A SNACK 5. GRAEME POSING IN HIS BEDROOM 6. I'VE ALWAYS THOUGHT 2 HEADS ARE BETTER THAN 1! 7. TORTOISE SHELL INSPIRED WOODEN BOWL 8. GRAEME'S CENTRAL FREE-STANDING BATH 9. LUCKY BUGGER CAN ENJOY THE VIRGINIA AIR SHOW FOR FREE 10. GARLIC & FETA HERB BALLS… DELISH! 11. DERYCK HEALEY'S MICROCOSM PAINTING 12. TERRAZZO KITCHEN FLOOR 13. GIGLEE PRINT BY DERYCK HEALEY 14. THIS IS A NECESSITY DURING DURBAN SUMMERS 15. BUDDHA GUARDING MARIANNE MEIJER'S PAINTING 16. PART OF DERYCK HEALEY'S SCULPTURE MADE FROM SHREDDED BANK NOTES.
For captions relevant to other pictures in this chapter, please refer to the Addendum.

LIMONCELLO

Graeme's love of Italian cooking took him to Marcella Hazan's cooking school on numerous occasions. The third time was to study bread making with Marcella's two assistants. "They were two old spinsters whose great grandparents had been bakers. They could not speak English but we had a fabulous week with them."

On his return to England, Graeme did an afternoon course with Italian food specialist, Ursula Ferrigno, and ended up swopping some of his newly acquired bread recipes for Ursula's Limoncello recipe. It was faxed to Graeme on her letterhead and was entitled, "My grandmother's Limoncello recipe" and signed, "Salute, Ursula."

10 large lemons (or 20 small lemons) • 250g castor sugar • 4 cups (1L) vodka

Remove the zest from the lemons and squeeze out all the juice. Place in a large bowl with the sugar and alcohol. Stir every other day. After 2 weeks, strain and bottle the liquid. Store the bottle in your fridge and serve ice cold.

MAKES 1L

 URSULA SAYS THAT YOU SHOULD IDEALLY USE AMALFI LEMONS WHICH HAVE A BIG PITH, BUT AFTER TASTING THIS SOUTH AFRICAN VERSION (TOO DELICIOUS), I'D SAY BIG, UNWAXED SA LEMONS CRACK THE NOD.

PARMESAN CUSTARD
with anchovy toast

This is one of Graeme's most cooked recipes and for good reason… it's fabulous. It's adapted from Rowley Leigh's recipe, *Le Café Anglaise* restaurant's chef, who is also the food writer for the *Financial Times*. It is the runaway hit of his restaurant… I think you will concur.

1 cup (250ml) double cream
• 1 cup (250ml) milk • 100g Parmesan, grated finely • 4 egg yolks
• salt & pepper to taste • cayenne pepper • 50g unsalted butter
• 12 anchovy fillets • 8 thin slices of crisp toast

Mix the cream, milk and Parmesan in a bowl and warm it gently over a pan in boiling water until the cheese has melted. Allow to cool completely. Whisk in the egg yolks, salt, pepper and cayenne pepper. Lightly butter 8 small ramekins of about 80ml and pour in the mixture. Place the moulds into a pan of boiling water and bake in an oven preheated to 150℃, until the mixture has set. Mash the anchovies and butter into a smooth paste and spread over the toast. Serve the anchovy toast alongside the mould on a plate.

SERVES 8

DID YOU KNOW THAT ANCHOVIES ARE THE MAIN INGREDIENT IN WORCESTERSHIRE SAUCE?

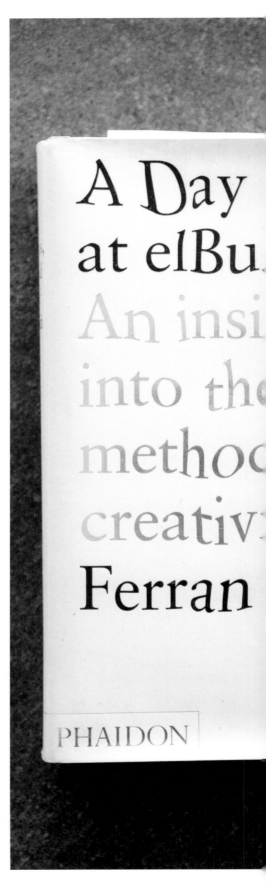

A Day
at elBu
An insi
into the
method
creativi
Ferran

PHAIDON

i

ht

ideas,

and

y of

Adrià

RUOTE WITH BOEREWORS
& yellow pepper sauce

This is adapted from Marcella Hazan's recipe, which uses what she calls "sweet sausages", but substituting traditional South African boerewors is perfect. If you were in Italy, you'd use Luganega sausages which, Graeme explains, "…are pure minced pork, possibly with a little lemon rind."

At the 9th Avenue International Food Festival in NYC, I tried Italian sausages, which tasted of fennel… "Aaaah" explains Graeme, "that's because most of the Italian immigrants arrived from Sicily, where fennel is standard in their sausages." Graeme certainly knows his sausages, and it's also a great opportunity to use the Cartwheel pasta… kids love it!

4 yellow peppers • 4T olive oil
• 1 large onion, chopped finely
• 300g boerewors, cut into 1cm rounds
• salt & pepper to taste • 1 tin (410g)
tomatoes • 1pkt (500g) ruote or rigatoni
pasta, cooked al dente

for tossing the pasta:
15g butter
• 90g Parmesan, grated

Deseed the peppers and cut the flesh into 2½cm squares. Place the olive oil and chopped onion into a sauté pan and cook on medium high, until the onion becomes golden. Add the sausages and cook for about 2 minutes. Then add the peppers and cook for approximately 8 minutes. Add salt, pepper and the chopped, tinned tomatoes. Cook at a medium heat until the oil and the tomatoes separate, stirring occasionally. Empty the contents of the pan over the cooked, drained pasta and toss thoroughly. Add the butter and Parmesan and toss again.
Serve with extra Parmesan on the table.

SERVES 4

BOEREWORS IS AN INHERITANCE FROM OUR PIONEERING FOREFATHERS. ANY OF THE RAW BOEREWORS THAT WASN'T EATEN WAS HUNG AND DRIED (DROËWORS) AND EATEN FOR SUSTENANCE DURING THE REST OF THEIR TREK.

CHICKEN FRICASSÉED

with rosemary & lemon juice

This is the simplest recipe, but proved a huge hit with my kids (8 and 12) who were with us as we prepared the food for the shoot. Graeme prefers thighs, although you could use a whole chicken. "The secret is to keep the lid of the pan askew as it cooks, so the moisture is contained while the chicken steams…" adds a very sagacious Graeme.

8 chicken thigh pieces • 2T olive oil • a few sprigs of rosemary • 4 garlic cloves, peeled • salt & pepper to taste • 150ml dry white wine • 2T lemon juice, freshly squeezed • julienned peel of ½ a lemon

Wash the chicken in cold water and dry with a tea towel. Pour the oil into a large sauté pan and turn the heat up to medium high. Add the chicken, skin side down. Brown the chicken pieces on both sides, then add the rosemary, garlic, salt and pepper. Stir to mix. Add the wine and let it bubble for approximately 20 seconds to deglaze the pan. Turn the heat down to low and place the lid slightly ajar on top. Cook for 30-40 minutes, turning the pieces over occasionally until the meat is soft. If necessary, add water to keep the pan from drying out. Turn the heat up to high and add the lemon juice and rind pieces. Cook for about 30 seconds more and serve. Yay!

SERVES 4

THE CHICKEN IS THE CLOSEST LIVING RELATIVE OF THE TYRANNOSAURUS-REX.

HOLIDAY **HOME**

L-R: 1. QUAIL EGGS 2. MORE OF DERYCK HEALEY'S WORK IN GRAEME'S DRESSING ROOM 3. A WATCHFUL BUDDHA IN THE MAIN BEDROOM 4. THE LIVING ROOM OF GRAEME'S BACHELOR PAD 5. HOUSE & LEISURE MAGAZINE CLIPPING OF GRAEME'S PREVIOUS HOME 6. ANYONE UP FOR A DATE? *OPPOSITE:* GRAEME'S MINIMALIST BEDROOM DESIGNED BY ARCHITECT JOY BRASSLER

SPAGHETTINI

with crayfish

For this recipe, I was personally tasked to get fresh crayfish and ended up watching the last two crays being fished out of the tank, weighed and then taken away for the slaughter. Hmmm, one day I may just turn veggie… but, until then, this is a sexy dish for special occasions. Every time I have eaten pasta with Graeme, I am always delighted that the sauce just barely coats the pasta. This is the way pasta should be eaten… not laden with tons of sauce.

**4T olive oil • 1 large onion, chopped
• 2 garlic cloves, chopped finely
• 1 tin (410g) tomatoes, chopped • salt &
pepper to taste • 1 hot chilli
• 3 crayfish • 1 handful of parsley,
chopped • 1pkt (500g) spaghettini,
cooked al dente**

Place 3T olive oil and onion in a sauté pan on medium heat and cook until golden. Stir in garlic and cook for about 30 seconds. Add the chopped tin of tomatoes, salt, pepper and chilli to taste. Turn the heat down.

Break off the crayfish heads and cut them in half lengthways. Place them in the sauce flesh side down. Simmer for approximately 20 minutes until the oil separates from the sauce. Remove the flesh from the crayfish tails and cut it into pieces about 2-3cm in size. Remove the heads from the sauce, scraping off as much sauce as possible. Stir in the parsley. Stir in the crayfish tailpieces and cook for roughly 1-2 minutes. Mix the finished crayfish sauce into the cooked spaghettini, drizzle over 1T olive oil and toss together.

SERVES 4

TIP FROM GRAEME ON HOW TO COOK PASTA:
Bring a huge amount of water to the boil with the lid on. When the water comes to the boil, throw in a handful of salt. "It should taste like the sea". Bring back to the boil, throw in the pasta and stir once. Put the lid back on. When the water comes back to the boil, remove the lid again and stir to stop the pasta from sticking. Boil at a fast pace until al dente. Drain immediately, removing as much water as possible and mix into your sauce.

Do not rinse with water. Do not add olive oil to the water while cooking. Do not pour some olive oil over the cooked pasta to stop it from sticking together, as you want the pasta to absorb the sauce and not the olive oil.

STRAWBERRY ICE-CREAM

You'll need an ice-cream maker for this one. A lot of homemade ice-creams are made with eggs, which really aren't that nice. Try this one instead…

250g fresh strawberries
• 160g caster sugar • 200ml cold water
• 100ml double cream, cold

Remove the stalks from the strawberries and wash in cold water. Place the strawberries, the sugar and 200ml cold water in the food processor and blend until smooth. Whip the cream until it thickens slightly and add it to the strawberry mix. Pour all the contents into your ice-cream maker and follow the manufacturer's instructions.

SERVES 6

LEGEND HAS IT THAT THE ROMAN EMPEROR NERO USED TO SEND HIS SLAVES SCURRYING TO THE MOUNTAINS TO COLLECT SNOW AND ICE TO MAKE FLAVOURED ICES, THE PRECURSORS TO ICE-CREAM, IN THE FIRST CENTURY.

CHERRY CLAFOUTIS

This recipe has a bit of a legacy. It came from a friend of Graeme and Deryck's, who moved to the UK from SA, studied catering at Bournemouth College and then did a 3-month stint in Tours, Northern France where this recipe originated.

"It's a fatless sponge combined with a hot syrup which binds as the cake cooks". You can use other fruit but as Graeme says, "There's nothing quite like a cherry!"

1 tin (420g) of cherries or 2 punnets of fresh cherries • a little butter for the cake tin

mixture 1:
100g flour • 200g granulated sugar • 2 eggs • 1t baking powder • 2T milk • 1t vegetable oil • a pinch of salt • ½t vanilla essence

mixture 2:
150g sugar • 150g unsalted butter, softened • 2 eggs

Preheat the oven to 180°C. Place cherries (fresh or drained from tin) to cover the bottom of a buttered 23cm cake tin. Blend "mixture 1" in a blender until smooth and pour over the cherries. Blend "mixture 2" until smooth and pour over "mixture 1" in the cake tin. Bake in the preheated oven for an hour until the cake is set. Invert the cake onto a serving platter and serve warm.

SERVES 8

"IF LIFE IS A BOWL OF CHERRIES, THEN WHAT AM I DOING IN THE PITS?" - ERMA BOMBECK

SWISS CHARD TORTA
(spinach tart)

This was the first of Graeme's meals that I tasted when he was the guest chef at *Bean Bag Bohemia* restaurant. It was the vegetarian starter option and highly recommended for meat lovers too.

1½kg Swiss chard (or spinach) • 4 cups (1L) water • 2t salt • 1 large onion, chopped finely • 4T olive oil • 120g Parmesan, freshly grated • 2 lightly beaten eggs • 4T pine nuts • 6T seedless raisins, soaked in warm water • black pepper to taste • 80g breadcrumbs, lightly toasted

Cut the stems off the Swiss chard (spinach) and discard. Shred the leaves and wash in cold water. Bring 1L of water to the boil in a large pot. Add 2t salt and when the water boils, add the Swiss chard. Cook for roughly 15 minutes until tender. Drain and set aside to cool.

When cool, squeeze the chard between your hands to remove as much moisture as possible. Chop very finely. Preheat the oven to 180°C. On a medium heat, using a large sauté pan, cook the chopped onions in olive oil until golden. Add the chopped chard and cook on a medium heat. Cook until all the moisture has been removed from the Swiss chard, stirring frequently. Set aside and cool to room temperature.

Then add the grated Parmesan, beaten egg, pine nuts and drained, dried raisins. Season with salt and pepper to taste. Mix together until all the ingredients are evenly combined.

Smear the bottom inside of a 24-25cm loose-bottomed baking tin with 3T olive oil and coat the entire inside of the tin with breadcrumbs. Add the Swiss chard mixture, levelling it without pressing on it.

Top with the remaining breadcrumbs and drizzle with 1T olive oil. Bake in the preheated oven for 40 minutes. Remove the sides of the tin from the tart, making sure they don't stick. After 5 minutes slide the torta onto a serving platter and serve at room temperature.

SERVES 4-6

it's so beautifully arranged on the plate - you know someone's fingers have been all over it.

- JULIA CHILD

GRAEME'S TAKE ON...

A FOOLPROOF DISH: I know everyone can make a puttanesca, but I have never had a complaint about mine...

THE CONTENTS OF HIS FRIDGE: I keep all my perfumes (Aqua Di Parma, Aesop) in my fridge next to the Sicilian bottaga (grey mullet roe, fished from one small Sicilian bay).

HIS MOST MEMORABLE MEALS: I have eaten at restaurants (in both Paris and London) that only serve foie gras! Ferran Adrià's *La Terrasse* in Madrid was superb... the 12 courses at *Tetsuya's* in Sydney were memorable, but my best meal was the 14 courses at *Tom Aikens* in London. It was extraordinary and faultless... even when we said no to coffee, 5 extra dishes arrived (in test tubes!).

WHAT HE'D LIKE MOST TO SHOW GUESTS OF OUR COUNTRY: Christmas Bay (30 minutes drive north of Durban). Because it's the most beautiful, unspoilt beach I've ever been to! I grew up there and have such fond memories of it.

HIS NEXT FOODIE DESTINATION: I am celebrating my 60th birthday with quite a few trips, including Yountville in California, where *The French Laundry* is. The whole town is filled with great restaurants.

HIS MOST MEMORABLE AND CHALLENGING COOKING EXPERIENCE: For my mother's 70th birthday party, I made crespelle (pancakes) with green bacon (unsmoked bacon) and Swiss chard for 70 people, and followed this with poussin (baby chicken), which I had to cook in 4 different people's houses in Umhlali. Between the courses I drove to the homes to collect them... and dessert was my Venetian carrot cake and homemade ice-cream.

MARCELLA HAZAN'S COOKING CLASSES: She's feisty and doesn't suffer fools. Her classes are completely informative with only 6 people per class. The classes are also very interactive... like how to debone a sardine!!! One day is market day... you are shown how to pick the right zucchini and fresh fish... and then you head off to *Da Fiore* restaurant, a highlight with 12 courses of seafood... it's got an exotic selection, like canocchie (mantis shrimp)!

HIS FAVOURITE SEAFOOD DISH: Sea bass is considered by the Italians to be the finest fish. I buy mine from the *Company Shed* in Essex (they are caught in the channel off the coast of Essex). I debone it and stuff it with mussels, prawns, breadcrumbs and bake it. You can then slice it. Mmm...

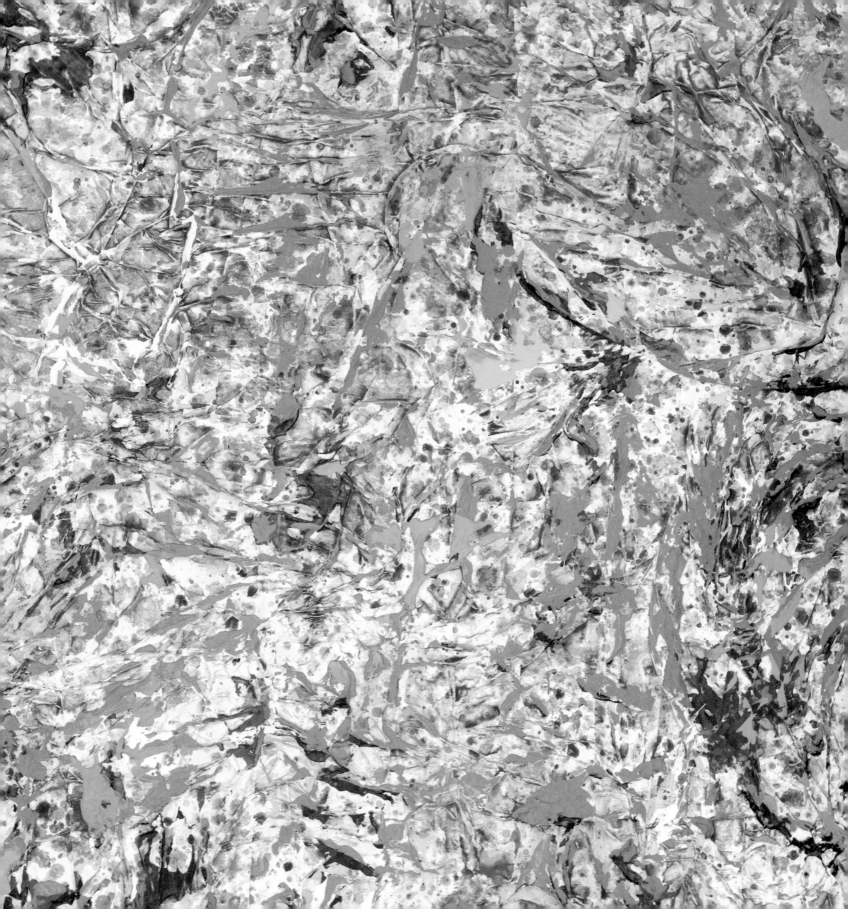

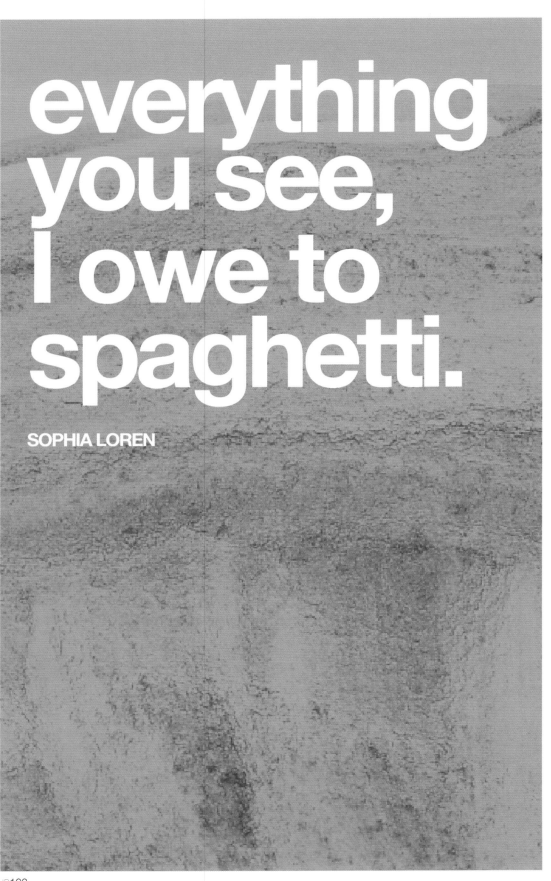

everything you see, I owe to spaghetti.

SOPHIA LOREN

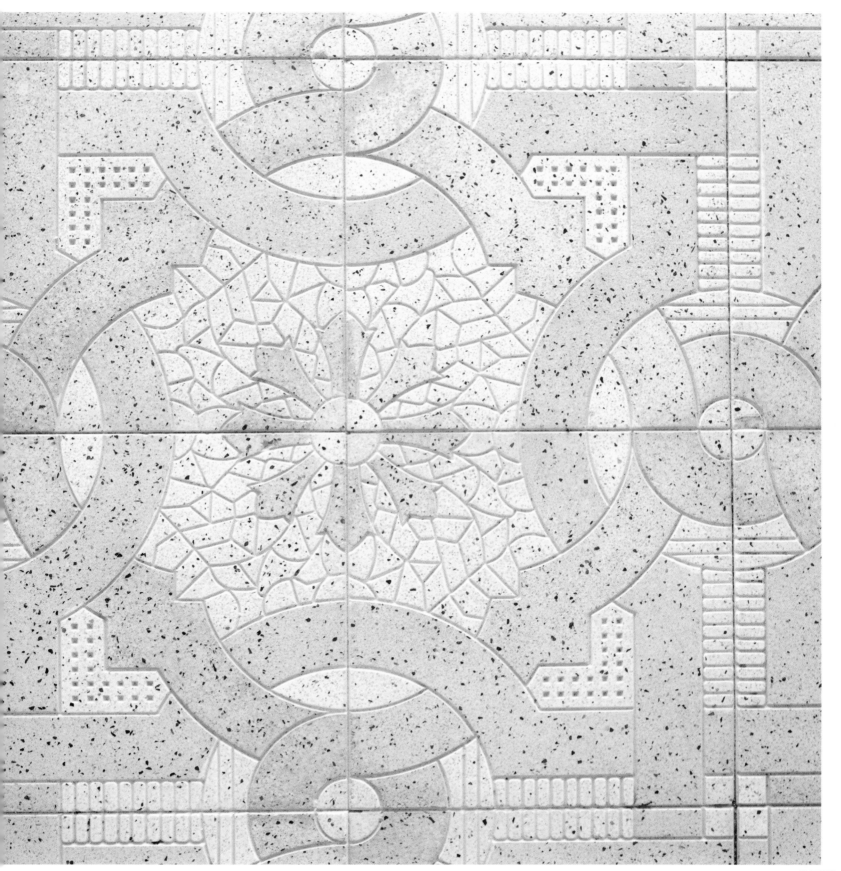

SHP**103**

MENU

opa's potato salad
prawn cocktail
the Bennetts' best ever cheese fondue
ostrich ragù lasagne
Dozza's beef wellington
breakfast in bread
mum's lemon meringue pie
grapefruit & rosewater jelly
heisse liebe (hot love)
pink martini

cape town

Nikki and Brandon

"HUNTERS AND GATHERERS", THAT'S WHAT I CALL NIKKI WERNER AND BRANDON DE KOCK. BRANDON, AKA BOND, AS EDITOR OF *COMPLEAT GOLFER*, HUNTS DOWN THE BEST GOLF COURSES IN THE WORLD (WHAT A JOB) AND NIKKI, AS FOOD EDITOR FOR *FAIRLADY*, GATHERS THE BEST RECIPES FOR A LOYAL AUDIENCE OF SOUTH AFRICAN FOOD LOVERS.

But their finely attuned hunting and gathering skills are most apparent when you enter their home. Collectively they seemed to have hunted and gathered every vintage bric-a-brac that vaguely echoes the crazy, hazy days of the '50s and '70s. Now that may sound like… well, like the olden days… but I was born in the '60s and lived a fab youth in the '70s listening to Bowie, lying on shaggy carpets and playing 8 tracks… so when I stepped into their home it was like a wave of nostalgia wafting over me.

If their eclectic home décor wasn't enough, Nikki also threw in another layer of accessories relating to her German heritage. Their home (it's more like a museum) belonged to Nikki's German grandparents and they worked with much of the existing furniture because it appealed to their retro sensibilities. Needless to say, Nikki loves vintage cookbooks and all food retro. My first amiable conversation with the pair flitted between knackwurst and bratwurst but, no matter what, I could not convince Bond to pull out the hidden lederhosen and show

me his moves. Maybe if I'd had access to an Oom-pah band, things would've been different. Brandon's dubbed 'Bond' for his ability to mix a mean martini and solve problems with general suaveness. Like the pink pinboard that he whipped up for Nikki to hang her kitchen utensils on. (What a find Nikki, not only can the man play golf and cook, he also does DIY… hold on to that man, hold on…) When I asked Bond how he had enhanced or changed their home, his answer was succinct: "Yes of course - home is the only gallery that will hang my photos!"

To be honest, I arrived at Nikki and Bond's home a little under the weather after a red letter night on the tiles… and the first thing we shot was the lemon meringue pie (definitely the best version ever). Who says that the Red Ambulance (Coca-Cola) is the best thing (next to a fry up) to cure a hangover? One slice of this pie and you'll have enough energy and voomah to… start all over again! That's how damn fine it is. And as for the "Hot Love"… you just gotta dip in, tuck in and get stuck in.

1. TEACUP SET FROM NIKKI'S OMA 2. MY NEW HANGOVER CURE! 3. MOBILE ORIGAMI FISH MADE BY BRANDON FROM *WALLPAPER* MAGAZINE ADVERT 4. FAREWELL GIFT FROM EX-NEIGHBOURS, ERIC & USHI 5. 'SUMMER WEEDS' CUSHION BY HEATHER MOORE 6. COFFEE POT GIVEN TO NIKKI BY HER FRIEND, LAUREEN 7. BOND KNOWS HOW TO KEEP HIS WOMAN HAPPY WITH THIS DIY KITCHEN UTENSIL HANGER! 8. VINTAGE COOKBOOK FROM ALNA & PHILIPPA 9. LOOKING PRETTY IN PINK! 10. SINGLE ORIGIN CHOCOLATE BUTTONS ON TOP OF OMA'S RECIPE CARD HOLDER 11. A GIFT FROM BRANDON'S FOLKS FROM THE KRUGER PARK WHEN HE WAS 10 YRS OLD! 12. PINK DAHLIAS PAINTING BY TRETCHIKOFF 13. CARLTONWARE SUGAR BOWL FROM NIKKI'S OMA 14. NIKKI'S BEST CHRISTMAS GIFT EVER 15. VINTAGE PUDDING BOWLS 16. BRANDON'S ORIGAMI MOUSE, DESIGNED BY ERIC JOISEL. *For captions relevant to other pictures in this chapter, please refer to the Addendum.*

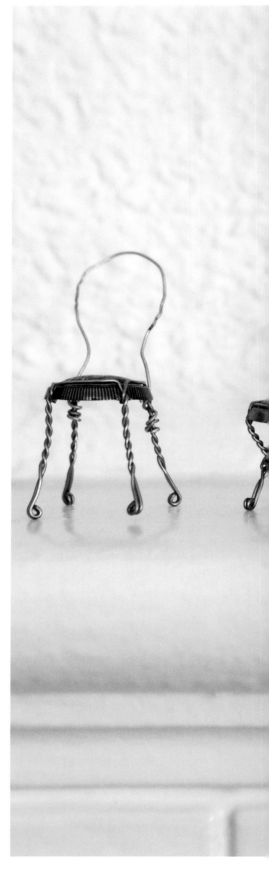

OPA'S POTATO SALAD

This is a tribute to Nikki's Swabian Opa because he always made this potato salad for Sunday lunch when she was growing up. Nikki: "It's real comfort food for me. Unlike the mayo, gherkin and boiled egg varieties I tasted for the first time at friends' braais, this one is made the traditional German way with vinaigrette and sliced, boiled, waxy potatoes. This salad is always on our Christmas table and I eat it as often as I can with bratwurst and German mustard – the kind that comes in a jar shaped like a beer mug."

for the salad:
1kg Mediterranean potatoes
• ½ English cucumber
• 1t salt • 1t sugar • ⅓ cup (80ml) sunflower oil • ⅓ cup (80ml) spirit vinegar • ⅓ cup (80ml) water
• salt & white pepper to taste

to serve:
bratwursts & knackwursts, simmered, fried or grilled • hot German mustard

Tip the potatoes into a large pot, cover with cold water, place the lid on top and bring to the boil. Once the water starts boiling, remove the lid, turn down the heat and simmer until the potatoes are tender but not falling apart (about 20 minutes). In the meantime, peel and thinly slice a cucumber and place it in a sieve. Sprinkle over salt and sugar and leave to draw the juices out of the cucumber. Drain the potatoes and when cool enough to handle (but still warm), peel off the skins and slice, not too chunky but also not so thin that they break up.

Place the potato slices in a large bowl. Mix together the oil, vinegar and water and pour over the potatoes. Sprinkle generously with salt and pepper, add the cucumber and toss well using your hands. (The potatoes must be warm when you dress them so that they absorb some of the dressing.) Set aside for an hour and serve with bratwursts, knackwursts and mustard.

SERVES 4-6

PRAWN COCKTAIL

Nikki: "I made this from *The Prawn Cocktail Years* for my mum's 60th birthday dinner and the biggest compliment I received was when she grabbed my arm as I was clearing and said, 'Nikki, it was better than the Plaza Espania circa 1969."

for the mayonnaise:
2 egg yolks • 1t Dijon mustard
• sea salt flakes & white pepper for
seasoning • 1 cup (250ml) sunflower oil
• ½ lemon, juiced

Whisk together the egg yolks, mustard and a good pinch of salt and pepper. While whisking continuously, gradually pour in the oil in a thin and steady stream until it comes together to form the mayonnaise. Season with lemon juice and more salt and pepper if necessary. Thin out with a little boiling water if it's too thick.

for the marie-rose sauce:
½ cup (125ml) homemade mayonnaise
• 2T tomato sauce • a few shakes of
Tabasco sauce • 2t brandy • spritz of
lemon juice

Mix together the mayonnaise, tomato sauce, Tabasco, brandy and lemon juice.

to serve:
1 iceberg lettuce, shredded • 2 spring
onions, topped and tailed, sliced finely
• ¼ cucumber, peeled, deseeded and
diced finely • 400g cooked and peeled
prawns (Giovanni's sell brilliant
quality prawns... ready for a prawn
cocktail) • ice

Lightly toss together the cucumber, lettuce and spring onion and divide between the top halves of four prawn cocktail glasses. Fill the bases of the prawn cocktail glasses with ice and place the glass bowls on top. Arrange the prawns on top of the lettuce mix and spoon the sauce over the prawns.

SERVES 4

L-R: 1. CERAMIC BAMBI SALT & PEPPER SET 2. BOND'S HOME ASSEMBLED PAPERCRAFT 1:1 ASSAULT RIFLE AK 47, DESIGNED BY MARTIN POSTLER 3. ANOTHER VINTAGE COOKBOOK 4. OMA'S OLD OVEN GLOVE 5. THIS TIN STORES NIKKI & HER MUM'S HOMEMADE SPICED GERMAN CHRISTMAS BISCUITS 6. NIKKI & BRANDON ENJOYING THE FRUITS OF THEIR LABOUR *OPPOSITE:* OLD SCHOOL IS NEW SCHOOL!

THE BENNETTS' BEST-EVER CHEESE FONDUE

Nikki: "There are always shot glasses of Kirsch, slices of bockwurst, Granny Smith apples, pickled onions and cubed baguette alongside the fondue. I was taught how to make it when living in Australia (of all places) by a friend's father, Peter Mayhew, who never missed his annual ski break. Peter, who got this recipe from his skiing family friends (the Bennett's), also taught me that the Kirsch is vital for digestion. So we first dip the piece of baguette in the Kirsch before submerging it in the bubbling cheese."

for the fondue:
1 garlic clove • 1½ cups (375ml) white wine • 350g Gruyere cheese, grated • 350g strong cheddar, grated • 2T cornflour or maizena • 3T Kirsch (cherry brandy) • pinch of paprika or freshly grated nutmeg

to serve:
1 baguette, cubed • 4 bockwurst, cooked and sliced thickly • 1 Granny Smith apple, cubed • 16 pickled onions, halved • 24 boiled baby potatoes, halved

Rub the inside of a thick pottery dish with garlic. (You can prepare the fondue in an ordinary pot and then transfer it to a fondue pot - I make mine in my cast-iron fondue pot on the stovetop and then transfer it to the burner.) Add wine to the pot and heat to boiling point but NOT bubbling. This is the secret - if your wine is too hot the cheese will never incorporate!
Add all the grated cheese GRADUALLY, stirring constantly. Mix the cornflour into the Kirsch and add to the cheese mixture. Keep cooking and stirring for 3-4 minutes. You can add grated nutmeg or paprika. Keep stirring all the time, people! Serve with French bread (and other accompaniments) and serve the same wine as was used in the fondue. In Zurich they give each guest a small glass of Kirsch in which to dip the bread before it goes into the fondue and this practice is highly recommended!

SERVES 8

OSTRICH RAGÙ LASAGNE

Brandon: "The secret to a 'good' lasagne is clearly defined layers of sheet pasta separated by thin layers of intense ragù and béchamel. 'Good' lasagne should stand up invitingly on your plate, not slide away. I love Giorgio Locatelli's version. He's more interested in method than recipe and Italian cooking is all about drawing maximum flavour out of minimum ingredients!"

for the ragù:
2T olive oil • 1 celery stalk, chopped finely • 1 carrot, chopped finely • 1 large onion, chopped finely • 2 garlic cloves, chopped finely • a sprig of rosemary • 2 sage leaves • 500g well-seasoned ostrich mince • 1 cup (250ml) red wine • 2T tomato paste • 1 cup (250ml) tomato purée • 1 cup (250ml) water

Heat up the oil on a very low heat in a big pot. Finely chop the celery, carrot, onion and garlic and chuck them in the pot. Add the herbs, tied together in a little parcel. Put on the lid and leave the veg to sweat it out (as long as 15 minutes). When it's all soft and gooey, remove and set aside. Turn up the heat and when the pot's hot, add the mince. Spread it around the bottom of the pot and leave to sizzle for about 5 minutes. Then chuck the veggies back in and stir it around. After about 10 minutes, the mince will start sticking to the bottom of the pot. Now it's thirsty for the wine - pour in the wine and let it evaporate completely. Add the tomato paste and stir vigorously for 1-2 minutes. Now add the tomato purée and water. Bring to the boil, then turn down the heat to low and leave to simmer for about 1 hour (the longer the better!). When it's ready, it should be a nice, thick sauce.

to assemble the lasagne:
béchamel sauce (see *addendum* for recipe) • 1pkt (500g) lasagne sheets • ostrich ragù • Parmesan, grated

Get a big pot of water ready to parboil the lasagne sheets as you assemble the layers - about 3-4 minutes. Take a suitably sized dish and start off with a ladle of béchamel on the bottom. Place a layer of pasta sheets down and, on top of that, spread a thin layer of ragù, then drizzle over a thin layer of béchamel. Finish off the layer with a light grating of Parmesan before taking the next semi-cooked pasta sheets out the pot. Lay them down over the mixture. Keep going until you're finished. About 4-5 layers is perfect. The trick is to keep the layer mixture quite sparse or thin. (You should have plenty leftover mince for bolognaise.) When you've laid the last sheets down, cover with béchamel and sprinkle with grated Parmesan. Put into a 180°C preheated oven for about half an hour, until the Parmesan crisps up. For my money, this style of lasagne gets better and better each time it's reheated. SERVES 4

DOZZA'S BEEF WELLINGTON

Brandon: "There's something quite magical about slicing open a Welly and getting hit with the earthy aromas rising up from contrasting layers of ochre, deep brown and velvety pink. Yum. When my English mate, Dozza, said he hadn't had a decent Wellington in SA, I couldn't resist the challenge. I got it right on the second attempt. Dozza has no reason to sugarcoat the truth, and he reckoned it's the best he's ever had. That's good enough for me."

1kg beef fillet • salt & pepper for seasoning • 50g butter • 1T sunflower oil • 2 shallots, chopped • 20g dried porcini, soaked in 100ml boiling water • 2t fresh thyme leaves, chopped • 2t garlic, crushed • 250g portobellini mushrooms, cleaned & chopped roughly • 150ml dry white wine • 1T chopped parsley (dried very well after washing) • 2 x 80g packs Parma ham slices • flour for dusting • 2 x 500g ready-rolled frozen puff pastry, defrosted • 1 egg, beaten (for glazing)

Tie up the beef so that it's an even thickness throughout. Season the beef well. Melt half the butter and 1T sunflower oil in a large, heavy based frying pan over a high heat. When foaming, brown the fillet all over for about 5 minutes. Set aside. Melt the rest of the butter in another frying pan. Add the shallots and sauté until softened. Drain the porcini and wash well to get rid of any grit, then add to the pan with the thyme, garlic and portobellini mushrooms. Strain the porcini liquid (also for any sand or dirt), add to the pan and cook the mushrooms until they are broken down and 'sticky'. Pour in the white wine, season, and reduce until all the wine has evaporated and the mixture is almost dry. Transfer it to a food processor, together with the parsley, and process until you have a "pâté" consistency. Set aside.

*FOR THE REST OF THE BEEF WELLINGTON RECIPE, REFER TO THE ADDENDUM.

SERVES 6

BREAKFAST IN BREAD

Brandon came up with this one idle Sunday afternoon: olive oil dough studded with crispy fried bacon bits and caramelised onion. It is heaven, fresh from the oven… spread with fresh butter or top with a fried egg for a complete breakfast. (We always use our trusty pink KitchenAid to do the dirty work and knead the dough.)

200g streaky bacon rashers • 88ml extra-virgin olive oil • 2 red onions, sliced finely • 1t brown sugar • 500g strong bread flour • 20g coarse semolina • 1pkt (10g) yeast • 10g sea salt flakes • 320ml water • flour for dusting

Slowly fry the bacon until crispy in a pan over a low heat, remove and set onto some paper towels. Then chop or crumble into pieces. Wipe out the frying pan with some paper towel and add 2T olive oil. Fry the onions until caramelised, adding a little brown sugar when they start to soften. Mix the bread flour, semolina, salt and yeast in a bowl. Add the olive oil and water. Hold the bowl with one hand and mix the ingredients around with the other for 2-3 minutes, until the dough starts to form. Tip the dough onto a clean work surface (do not add any flour even if the dough looks very moist) and knead the dough for about 10 minutes until it is smooth and elastic. Make a well in the centre, add the bacon and onion and knead until it comes together as a sticky dough. Place the dough in a lightly oiled bowl, cover with a clean tea towel and leave to rise in a warm, draught-free place for 1 hour. Tip the dough out of the bowl and onto a clean work surface, this time sprinkled with flour. Shape the dough into a ball. Return to the bowl and leave to rise for another 30 minutes. Tip out onto the floured surface again and shape the ball of dough into a large loaf by folding the edges under. Cut three slashes across the top with a sharp knife. Place the dough on a greased baking sheet and leave to rest for 30-60 minutes. Preheat the oven to 190°C. Gently go over the cuts on top of the bread with a sharp knife and bake the bread for 45 minutes. Allow to cool slightly and serve warm.

BOND SAYS

THE GREAT THING ABOUT MAKING YOUR OWN BREAD IS THAT ANYTHING GOES… ADD WHATEVER YOU LIKE AND FOLLOW THE BASIC METHOD. YOU CAN'T GO WRONG… JUST EXPERIMENT!

MUM'S LEMON MERINGUE PIE

Nikki's mum's lemon meringue pie recipe is originally from her neighbour, Bev McHutcheon, and it's one of those recipes that was shared while chatting over the garden fence. It's typically suburban SA with Tennis biscuits and condensed milk… Nikki: "What sold me is the unfailingly solid meringue crust - I can't bear those shrivelled-up, weeping specimens in home-bake shops." Brandon apparently always picks lemon curd over chocolate ganache, so Nikki bakes it every year as his birthday cake.

for the biscuit base:
1pkt Tennis biscuits, crushed
• 100g butter, melted

for the meringue topping:
2 egg whites, beaten until stiff
• 112g castor sugar

for the lemon filling:
1 large tin (385g) condensed milk
• ½ cup (125ml) fresh lemon juice
• 2 egg yolks

Preheat the oven to 230°C. Mix together the biscuit base ingredients and press into a 20cm cake tin or pie dish. Beat the egg whites and slowly add the caster sugar, then set aside in the fridge. Combine the filling ingredients and beat until smooth. Fill the biscuit base with the lemon filling and spoon over the meringue topping. Place the pie in the oven and immediately turn down the heat to 120°C. Bake for 30 minutes and then turn down the oven's temperature again to 100°C and bake for another hour. If time permits, turn the oven off and leave the pie in there to cool.

SERVES 6

DURING THE ERA OF LOUIS XIV, WOMEN USED LEMONS TO REDDEN THEIR LIPS.

GRAPEFRUIT & ROSEWATER JELLY

Developed for a food shoot, this pretty-in-pink jelly has an unexpected punchy citrus flavour and the scent of roses. It deserves to be set in a big, old-fashioned mould and turned out all shimmering and wobbly.

4 cups (1L) freshly squeezed juice from 6-8 ruby grapefruits • ½ cup (125ml) caster sugar • 12 leaves of Gelita gelatin (available from delis & good food stores) • 2t rosewater • vegetable oil for greasing

Strain the grapefruit juice into a saucepan and add the sugar. Bring to the boil, stirring to dissolve the sugar. Lay the gelatin leaves in a shallow bowl filled with some cold water and leave to soften for 5 minutes. Once the leaves have started to soften, quickly squeeze them out and place them into another bowl with some of the hot grapefruit juice. Whisk well until the gelatin is well combined with the grapefruit juice. Add this mixture to the rest of the grapefruit juice and stir well. Stir in the rosewater. Oil a large jelly mould, lightly but thoroughly, using some paper towel and vegetable oil. Pour the jelly into the mould and refrigerate until it is firmly set. To turn the jelly out of the mould, fill a shallow bowl with boiling water.

Then dip a cloth in the water and use it to wipe the outside of the mould thoroughly. Repeat this a few times and then place a serving plate on the underside of the mould and invert the jelly.

FILLS A LARGE 1L MOULD - SERVES 4

IT'S SAID THAT GRAPEFRUIT GOT ITS NAME BECAUSE IT GROWS LIKE GRAPES IN CLUSTERS. ONE CLUSTER CAN HAVE UP TO 25 GRAPEFRUITS.

HEISSE LIEBE
(hot love)

"I adore the name of this dessert," says Nikki. "It's a hot, black cherry and raspberry sauce served over scoops of vanilla ice-cream in old-fashioned ice-cream glasses. Made complete by dollops of whipped cream and triangular wafers wedged in the side, it is so easy but a delight to eat. It's the dessert of choice when my southern German family heads to their favourite restaurant, the Heldenberg, to celebrate birthdays and special occasions."

for the 'hot love' sauce:
150g fresh cherries • 1t Cointreau
• 40g castor sugar
• 150g fresh raspberries

to serve:
quality vanilla ice-cream • whipped cream • 8 vanilla wafers

Rinse the cherries, remove the stalks and pit. Tip into a saucepan along with any residual juices from the board. Add the Cointreau and sugar and simmer gently until the sugar is dissolved. Push the raspberries through a sieve and add to the cherries. Stir to warm through and remove from the heat. (You could keep some raspberries back and add them to the sauce just before serving.) Place three scoops of vanilla ice-cream into a cold bowl, top with cream and add a wafer. Serve the warm sauce in a jug on the side for pouring over the ice-cream.

SERVES 4

 IF YOU KISS SOMEONE FOR ONE MINUTE YOU WILL BURN ROUGHLY 6-7 CALORIES.

PINK MARTINI

Very Bond, not quite a recipe but perfect for the theme… Nikki and Brandon shook up a batch of pink martini's last Valentine's Day, to the sounds of Pink Martini!

2 tots (50ml) vodka
- **½ tot (15ml) Crème de cassis**
- **½ tot (15ml) sweet vermouth**

to serve:
glacé cherries (with stalks)

Add the ingredients into a cocktail shaker with crushed ice and shake well. Strain the contents into a Martini glass and garnish with a cherry.

MAKES 1 MARTINI

NO ONE SEEMS TO KNOW FOR SURE HOW OR WHEN THE MARTINI WAS CREATED, BUT THE FIRST ITEM IN A MARTINI WAS A CHERRY.

BRANDON'S NUTS & BOLTS

ALIAS? Bond **HOW YOUNG?** 40 **MONEYMAKER?** Magazine Editor **YOU'D RATHER BE?** A barman - in an Amsterdam coffee shop **WHAT DOES IT FOR YOU?** Nix, folks, food, Irish whisky, sport **WHAT DOESN'T?** Brussel sprouts, liars, queues **WHERE'S YOUR FAVOURITE PLACE IN SA?** Cape Point lighthouse just before a storm **WHAT'S YOUR FAVOURITE PLACE IN THE WORLD?** New York City **WHERE DO YOU GO TO ESCAPE?** Arniston, in the Western Cape **GOT ANY HOBBIES/ PASSIONS?** Sport, cooking, origami, photography **WHAT'S YOUR FAVOURITE ITEM IN THE HOUSE?** Opa's old light fitting with the bond girl silhouettes **A MUST-SEE FOR GUESTS IN SA?** The paradox of modern African existence **HOW DO YOU INDULGE YOURSELF?** By spending huge amounts of ammo on experiences rather than things **WHAT SINGLE THING ABOUT YOUR HOME REFLECTS YOUR INDIVIDUALISM?** My library **IF YOUR ROOF WAS COMING DOWN ON TOP OF YOU, WHAT WOULD YOU GRAB ON THE WAY OUT?** The Ramblings of an Idiot - my sporadic collection of diaries over the past 25 years

NIKKI'S NUTS & BOLTS

ALIAS? Nix, princess, Joni (as in Mitchell) **HOW YOUNG?** 32 **MONEYMAKER?** Food Editor **YOU'D RATHER BE?** Full-time traveling foodie **WHAT DOES IT FOR YOU?** Bond, family, friends, travel, winter, early mornings, good coffee, proper bread with fresh butter, dark chocolate, slow cooking, most things vintage **WHAT DOESN'T?** The Southeasterly **WHERE'S YOUR FAVOURITE PLACE IN SA?** The West Coast and the Karoo **WHAT'S YOUR FAVOURITE PLACE IN THE WORLD?** Germany **WHERE DO YOU GO TO ESCAPE?** Overseas **GOT ANY HOBBIES/ PASSIONS?** Cooking, having friends around our table, the '50s & '70s, arty films **WHAT'S YOUR FAVOURITE ITEM IN THE HOUSE?** The pink pegboard Brandon built to hang up all my kitchen utensils **A MUST-SEE FOR GUESTS IN SA?** The lesser-known small towns and outer-lying areas that are quietly producing some pretty inspiring food and wine; Cape Town's awe-inspiring beaches that are in such close proximity to the city **HOW DO YOU INDULGE YOURSELF?** Spa, spa, spa **WHAT SINGLE THING ABOUT YOUR HOME REFLECTS YOUR INDIVIDUALISM?** The Alpine wall mural **IF YOUR ROOF WAS COMING DOWN ON TOP OF YOU, WHAT WOULD YOU GRAB ON THE WAY OUT?** Pink KitchenAid, red velvet and sparkly gold catsuits, laptop

1 GLASS MILK
170 CALORIES

1 OZ BACON
150 CALORIES

8 SHRIMP
116 CALORIES

1 FRIED EGG
130 CALORIES

300 CALORIES

APPLE
80 CALORIES

4 OZ CHEESE
240 CALORIES

6 STALKS
25 CALORIES

LETTUCE
48 CALORIES

2 PLUMS
40 CALORIES

JELLO 1 CUP
175 CALORIES

Calories

DANGER

1 SLICE
50 CALORIES

1 EGG
70 CALORIES

4 CALORIES

HOT DOG
250 CALORIES

20
90 CALORIES

BEEF STEAK
4 OZ
200 CALORIES

5
10 CALORIES

1 BANANA
100 CALORIES

½ CANTALOUPE
100 CALORIES

1 SLICE
75 CALORIES

I tell you one thing.
I've been to a parallel
universe, I've seen time
running backwards,
I've played pool with
planets, and I've given
birth to twins, but I
never thought in my
entire life I'd taste an
edible Pot Noodle.

CRAIG CHARLES

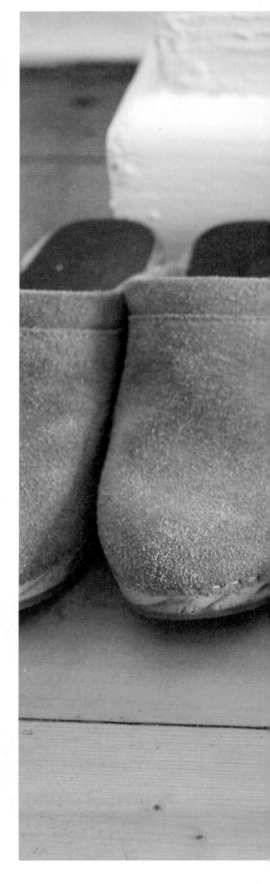

linseed bread rings
citrus salad with grilled duck breast
roast pepper salad
mozzarella balls baked in lemon halves
renaissance chicken liver pâté with thyme butter
wood-fired peri-peri prawns
roast fillet on a bed of sautéed shiitake mushrooms
roast venison with quince jelly & baked polenta
almond cake with fresh cherries

Russel AND Camilla

OBS: Cape Town

RUSSEL AND I GO WAAAY BACK… ALL THE WAY BACK TO HIS HOME TOWN OF DURBAN. I THINK WE MET IN BARS AND DRANK ICE COLD JUGS OF BEER TOGETHER… YES, IT'S ALL COMING BACK TO ME, I'M SURE OF IT!

Russel began his working life as a copyjockey in an ad agency, moving on to run his own agency for 4 years. He contributed as a freelance entertainment and travel writer to various magazines too, but eventually his love for food, people and entertainment drew him into the idea of running a cigar bar in Durban, called *Cuban Pete's*. Late nights, sexy clientele and good food inspired the jack-of-all-trades to pick up a camera & shoot. Russ quickly specialised in food (his true love), following his new calling to Cape Town. His latest career is one he excels at and why he's one of the main photo guys for *Shiny Happy People*. There is another reason why I loved meeting up with Russ and shooting these pages. Her name is CAMILLA!

It's a strange thing that it took me so long to meet Camilla. From many different sources all I ever heard was, "You must meet Camilla! You'll love Camilla. Camilla will just love you!". As luck would have it, this book took us away together to Catherine Raphaely's farm, Vermaklikheid. I was mistaken, thinking the farm was like, 1 hour out of Cape Town… it was more like 5! Needless to say the long car trip was the perfect introduction to Camilla. We literally did not stop yakking and

eating junk food (except when we were yakking) for the entire road trip. Conversations swung from knitting to bird shooting, and included foie gras, Murray River Salt, pheasant, anecdotes about meeting Antonio Carluccio, her "almost love affair" with Marcella Hazan's son, her time spent as the personal chef to one of her parents' rich clients in Castle Rock, Colorado, cooking with Chinese chef Nancy Cox in San Francisco, and penis enlargements (but that's another story altogether)!

Camilla is a darling! She works in food development for *Woolworths*, but loves to cook and entertain. She also taught me how to make Hollandaise sauce (yes, I know, you would imagine that I could make Hollandaise, but I couldn't! But now that I can, it's a classic) and she also got me to do all the gross things in the kitchen, like de-vein all the tiger prawns (love you, Camilla), but it was worth it after Russell cooked them in his newly built wood-fired oven - his prized possession. With all the food being cooked there was only one thing left to do… eat it! And that's exactly what we did… with friends and red wine and very loud conversation in their warm and comforting Observatory home. I just loved it! Really loved it!

1. CAMILLA'S "WONKI WARE" CROCKERY 2. THE START OF A RENAISSANCE… FOR CHICKEN LIVER PÂTÉ 3. BOCCONCINI BALLS ABOUT TO BE BAKED 4. CAMILLA LOOOVES SWEET POTATOES 5. A GIFT FROM RHYS TO HIS "GEOGRAPHICALLY CHALLENGED" FRIEND, CAMILLA 6. LOTS OF LOVE IN THIS HOME! 7. LINSEED BREAD RINGS IN THE MIX 8. COLLECTION OF "EXPERIENCED" POTS 9. A HANDMADE QUILT FROM CAMILLA'S MOM 10. STAR-STRUCK CAMILLA POSING WITH HER FAVOURITE CHEF, ANTONIO CARLUCCIO 11. NOW THAT'S USING YOUR HEAD! 12. RUSSEL THE PRO PHO-TAG DOING HIS THANG 13. THEIR WOOD-FIRED OVEN MADE BY FIREOVEN 14. CAMILLA'S TRINKET BOX IS A CUSTOM-MADE WEDDING GIFT FROM FRIENDS 15. THE "FAMILY TRUST FUND" GIVEN TO RUSSEL AT THEIR WEDDING BY CAMILLA'S DAD 16. ONE OF CAMILLA'S KITCHEN INSPIRATIONS, HER GRANDMOTHER. *For captions relevant to other pictures in this chapter, please refer to the Addendum.*

LINSEED BREAD RINGS

There is one ingredient missing from this bread recipe that Camilla added especially for me. A super large pinch of truffle infused salt she had picked up on one of her travels to Europe on food related business. Camilla and I both wish we had truffles in the backyard and a trained pig to dig them out for us. Our idea of heaven…

4 cups (400g) cake flour • 1t sea salt • 1pkt (10g) instant yeast • 1 cup (250ml) milk • ½ cup (125ml) water • 3T olive oil • egg wash to coat the rings • 3T linseeds

Place the flour In a large bowl and mix in the salt. Sprinkle the yeast on top. Place the milk and water in a jug and heat in the microwave until luke warm before adding the olive oil.

Pour the wet mixture over the flour and yeast ingredients. Using your hands combine to form a firm dough. Turn out onto a clean surface and knead until the gluten is well developed. Return the dough to the bowl, cover and allow to double in size for 1½ hours.

Knock back and divide the dough into 16 individual pieces. Roll the pieces into a sausage and join the two ends to form doughnuts. Place the rings on a baking sheet, brush with egg wash and sprinkle with linseeds. Allow the dough to rise again for at least 30 minutes and bake in a 230°C preheated oven for 10 minutes. Then reduce the heat to 180°C and bake for a further 10 minutes. Remove from the oven and allow to cool before serving.

SERVES 8

LINSEED IS THE RICHEST SOURCE OF OMEGA-3 FATTY ACIDS AND CONTAINS ALMOST TWICE AS MUCH OMEGA-3 AS FISH OIL.

CITRUS SALAD

with grilled duck breast

Duck breast, unlike chicken, is perfectly delicious when cooked pink inside… in fact, insist on it. The combination of duck, citrus and the Asian-inspired dressing is quacking good (did I really say quacking?).

4 duck breasts • salt & pepper to season • 4 oranges • 3 pink grapefruit • 150g mixed Asian baby leaves • 100g cashew nuts, dry roasted • 6 spring onions, sliced thinly

**for the dressing:
4T soya sauce • 2cm knob ginger root, peeled and crushed • 3t sesame seed oil • 2t honey**

Score the skin of all 4 duck breasts and season with salt and pepper. Segment the oranges and grapefruit into a bowl and reserve all the squeezed juices and place in a saucepan. Add all the other dressing ingredients to the saucepan and bring to the boil, reduce the heat and allow to simmer until 1/3 of the liquid has evaporated. Remove and allow to cool.

Heat a pan on high and place the duck breasts, skin side down in the pan and cook for 3-4 minutes. Turn and repeat on the other side. Remove the duck breasts from the pan and allow to rest for 5-10 minutes while you assemble the salad.

Arrange a selection of Asian baby leaves on a platter. Add the orange and grapefruit segments, then sprinkle with cashew nuts and spring onions. Slice the duck breasts and arrange on the salad. Before serving, drizzle the dressing over the salad.

SERVES 4

DUCKS NEVER HAVE COLD FEET BECAUSE THEIR FEET DON'T HAVE ANY NERVES OR BLOOD VESSELS IN THEM.

L–R: 1. SCULPTURE BY RUSSEL'S BROTHER, MARTIN 2. ONE OF RUSSEL'S FASCINATING BOOKS ABOUT CRAZY FUNDAMENTALISM 3. CAMILLA'S "WONKI WARE" COLLECTION 4. THIS ROASTED PEPPER SALAD IS NOT FOR THE FAINT HEARTED 5. CAMILLA'S GRAN IN HER YOUTH 6. CAMILLA INSISTS ON GETTING HER PRODUCE FROM THE SHOP "WILD ORGANIC" *OPPOSITE:* TIGER PRAWNS ON A "WONKI WARE" PLATE

ROAST PEPPER SALAD

The use of the wood-fired oven is a winner when it comes to piling some veg into a pan and roasting them. Then Camilla, using her artful hand, turned them into a blazing good salad.

3 red peppers • 3 yellow peppers • 2 heads of garlic • a large sprig of rosemary • 2T olive oil • 2 rounds of feta cheese, cubed • 100g black calamata olives • 10 basil leaves • juice of 1 large lemon • pinch of sugar • freshly ground salt & pepper to season

Preheat the oven to 230℃. Quarter and deseed the peppers. Then place the quartered peppers, garlic heads and rosemary in a roasting dish and drizzle with olive oil. Roast in the oven uncovered for 20-30 minutes. Separate the peppers into a serving dish; squash the cloves of soft garlic out of the heads and mix into the peppers with the feta, olives and basil leaves. Dress with lemon juice, olive oil, sugar and season with salt and pepper.

SERVES 6-8

RUSSEL SAYS

SHE'S THE LOVE OF MY LIFE! THANKS SO MUCH TO RUDI & CHARL DE LANGE WHO CUSTOM-MADE MY BEAUTIFUL WOOD-FIRED OVEN. THEY'RE BROTHERS WHO SPECIALISE IN MAKING BREAD OVENS.

MOZZARELLA BALLS

baked in lemon halves

I confess that when I saw Russel's wood-fired oven I could not get beyond Jamie Oliver's Italian TV programme, where he stuffs mozzarella into lemon halves and then proceeds to incinerate them... our's weren't burnt at all and were totally delicious with the ground pink pepper corns. Salute Jamie, better luck next time!

2 lemons • 6 fresh bocconcini (Italian mozzarella cheese balls) • sea salt and freshly ground pink pepper corns to season • olive oil to drizzle • 4 bay leaves • 4 toothpicks

Preheat oven to 220°C or use a hot, wood-fired oven. Halve the lemons and gently squeeze out the juice. Using a spoon, remove most of the lemon segments to form an empty shell. Keep the lemon juice for the prawn recipe. Place the halved lemon "cups" in an ovenproof roasting pan. Place 1½ bocconcini in each lemon half, seasoning the cheese with salt and pink pepper, drizzle over some olive oil and seal the top half of the lemon with a bay leaf and tooth pick.

Bake in the oven for 15-20 minutes until the cheese is gooey and lightly golden. Serve with crusty bread or linseed rings.

SERVES 4

FOR CENTURIES THE UPPER CLASSES USED TOOTHPICKS MADE OF GOLD, SILVER OR IVORY AND INLAID WITH PRECIOUS STONES. A BODY OF ETIQUETTE GREW UP AROUND THE POPULAR TOOL'S USE, RESULTING IN BOOKS THAT ADVISED, "POKING AROUND THE TEETH DURING THE COURSE OF A MEAL" WAS A GRAVE OFFENSE.

RENAISSANCE CHICKEN LIVER PÂTÉ

with thyme butter

I have made tons of chicken liver pâté, but I have to give the *Shiny Happy People* award for the best pâté to Camilla. As Camilla said, "it's baked not fried", so in essence all the ingredients are liquidised and then baked in a buttered ceramic dish. Well done on the award Camilla! Gush! Gush!

250g free range chicken livers, cleaned • 1 cup (250ml) farm fresh cream • 3 eggs • ½ cup (125ml) port/sherry • 1t flaked sea salt • 2t black pepper, freshly ground • 1t (level) nutmeg, freshly ground • ½ cup (125ml) butter • a large sprig of thyme

Preheat the oven to 160℃. Place all the ingredients (except the butter and thyme) in a food processor and blend until smooth. Sieve and pour contents into a terrine dish. Place in a bain-marie (double-boiler) and bake for 45-50 minutes until the top of the pâté is golden brown and firm to the touch. While the pâté is baking, place the butter and thyme in a small saucepan and allow to infuse over a low heat. Once the pâté has cooled, pour the thyme-butter over the top and refrigerate until the butter has set.

SERVES 8-10

CAMILLA SAYS

WOW! THIS IS SO UNEXPECTED! I JUST WANT TO THANK MY MOM AND DAD, RUSSEL, MY GRANDMOTHER – WHO WAS AN INSPIRATION TO ME IN THE KITCHEN, MY POTS & PANS, THE DECEASED CHICKEN…

WOOD-FIRED PERI-PERI PRAWNS

On various trips to Mozambique, I was intrigued to learn how many recipes there are for peri-peri. It seems that anything with chillies, vinegar and olive oil goes. Seeing as I had to de-vein all the prawns, I most certainly ate my fair share of these wood-fired tigers.

for the concentrated peri-peri sauce:
20 chillies, medium-sized
• 10 garlic cloves • ½ cup (125ml) olive oil • ⅛ cup (30ml) white wine vinegar • 1t sea salt

Blend all the ingredients together to form a thick paste. Add extra olive oil if the paste is too thick and store in a sealed container in the fridge for later use.

for the prawns:
2kg large tiger prawns with heads
• water • 2T sea salt

Defrost the prawns and place them in some water with 2T sea salt and allow to rest for 30 minutes. Nancy Cox, a Chinese chef from San Francisco, taught Camilla that this "brings the sea back to the fish". Rinse and butterfly from head to tail and remove the nasty vein.

for the marinade:
2T sea salt • 125g melted butter
• 30ml olive oil • lemon juice of 2 lemons • 2T homemade peri-peri concentrate • 4 garlic cloves, crushed • 2t sea salt

Mix all the ingredients for the marinade together, pour it over the prawns and allow to rest in the fridge for 15 minutes. Place the marinated prawns on a large roasting pan and bake in the wood-fired oven for 6-8 minutes until they are firm to the touch and the prawns have turned pink. Alternatively you can grill them over a fire.

SERVES 6-8

ROAST FILLET

on a bed of sautéed shiitake mushrooms

In some instances, the farm girl in Camilla comes to the fore and the simplicity of great ingredients prepared simply comes bubbling out. Nothing wrong with a juicy piece of roast fillet and fresh shiitakes. Everybody loves a bit of beef, hey Camilla? (Nudge, Nudge, Wink, Wink!)

1 whole fillet, cleaned • 3-4t whole grain mustard • freshly ground black pepper to season • 150g of wild rocket • 2T (heaped) butter • 2 punnets shiitake mushrooms • flaked sea salt for seasoning • 4T balsamic vinegar • wedge of Parmesan for shavings

Preheat oven to 230°C, or the hottest setting you have. Remove the fillet from the fridge at least 1 hour prior to cooking to bring it to room temperature. Place the fillet on a baking tray and cover the top with the whole grain mustard and season with freshly ground black pepper. Roast the fillet in the oven for 20-25 minutes, then remove and leave it to rest for at least 15 minutes.

In the meantime, place the washed rocket on a large serving platter and set aside. Heat a large saucepan and melt the butter before tossing in the mushrooms. Season and cook over a high heat for about 5 minutes. Spoon the mushrooms onto the rocket; deglaze the pan with the balsamic vinegar. Slice the fillet and arrange it on the mushrooms. Cover the fillet with Parmesan shavings and finish with the balsamic dressing.

SERVES 6

IN ANCIENT TIMES IT WAS BELIEVED MUSHROOMS WERE CREATED BY THUNDERBOLTS BECAUSE WILD MUSHROOMS APPEAR AFTER STORMS.

ROAST VENISON WITH QUINCE JELLY
& baked polenta

Camilla grew up on a farm, she knows her way around wild things and insists that the best venison is well hung. This particular cut was wild bush pig baked with Membrillo, the Spanish paste that is made from the sour quince. A winner when served with the baked polenta.

1 leg of venison (bushpig), well hung • freshly ground sea salt & black pepper for seasoning • 3T olive oil • 5 medium onions, peeled and quartered • 2 large thumbs of fresh ginger root, peeled and crushed • 200ml sherry • 225g quince cheese

Preheat oven to 160℃. Season the leg roast with freshly ground sea salt and black pepper. Heat a large ovenproof casserole dish and add the olive oil. Brown the leg on all sides, remove and set aside. Put the onions and ginger root into the casserole dish and sauté, deglaze with the sherry. Return the browned leg to the casserole dish and place it on the bed of onions and ginger. Randomly place big dollops of Quince cheese all over and cover the casserole dish with a lid. Slow roast for 3-4 hours until the meat is tender and falling off the bone. Remove and carve the meat off the bone. Return to the meat juices, onions and ginger and serve with baked polenta and wilted greens.

for the baked polenta: 2 cups (500ml) milk • 2 cups (500ml) water • 180g yellow maize meal or polenta, ground • 3 eggs • 1t salt • freshly ground black pepper to season • 3T butter • 50g Parmesan, grated

Preheat the oven to 160℃. Heat the milk and water in a medium-sized saucepan. Just before it boils whisk in the maize meal. Whisk continuously to ensure there are no lumps, reduce the heat and allow to simmer on low for 15-20 minutes until the mixture is like thick porridge. Remove from the heat and whisk in all the other ingredients. Pour into an ovenproof dish and bake for 45 minutes until the dish is golden brown.

SERVES 6-8

ALMOND CAKE
with fresh cherries

I suggested to Camilla that she make this light almond cake as I had eaten it at one of her dinner parties. It's the perfect base to serve with a berry coulis, as it soaks up the sweet juices.

200g butter • 300g sugar • 6 eggs • 200g whole almonds, ground with skin on • pinch of salt • 90g cake flour • 50ml Kirsch or Amaretto liqueur • 250g punnet of fresh cherries • icing sugar for dusting

Preheat the oven to 180℃ and lightly grease a 20cm loose-bottom cake tin. Cream the butter and sugar together until light and fluffy. Add the eggs one at a time, beating well after each addition. Add the other ingredients (except the cherries and icing sugar) and blend until smooth. Spoon the mixture into the prepared tin and bake for 1 hour until the cake is a deep, golden brown and firm to the touch. Cool and remove the cake from its tin. Dust the cake with icing sugar and serve with fresh cherries. This is also delicious served with chocolate ice-cream.

SERVES 8-10

NEIL SAYS

TIP: THE CAKE'S FLAVOUR MATURES WITH TIME AND IT WILL KEEP IN AN AIRTIGHT CONTAINER FOR A WEEK!

cooking is like love. it should be entered into with abandon or not at all.

- HARRIET VAN HORNE

PROFILING RUSSEL

• **SIGN...** Sagittarius (an evolved one) • **LOVES...** Life, food, entertaining, profane language and my outdoor, wood-fired bread oven. • **HATES...** The waste of good ingredients in crap food, neckties, fake boobs, venues you can't wear jeans to, Nike swoosh tattoos (you aren't a billboard f**kwit!), poncy restaurants and religious fundamentalism. • **WHERE HE GOES TO ESCAPE...** If it was from a POW camp, I'd go through the tunnel like everyone else, but otherwise it's my studio. • **WHAT HIS HOBBIES/PASSIONS ARE...** I'm lucky enough to do what I love for a living - combining food, people and photography - but if you were being strict about nailing down a hobby, I would say it's cooking in my amazing wood-fired bread oven! • **THE MEAL HE'D SERVE A VISITOR IN SA...** People are always trying to force pap and wors, or bredie, or bobotie on foreigners, which is kak cos our culinary heritage is so diverse - from Malay, French, Zulu and English to Portuguese, Indian and Boer, you can choose from all of them. So I'd take a guest shopping at Salt River market for all the freshest ingredients, because that's what I think our real culinary strength is... amazing produce. • **HOW THEY REALLY, REALLY SPOIL THEMSELVES...** We invite a bunch of people around and cook something fabulous, then we try to keep everyone there for as long as possible. • **WHAT SINGLE THING IN THEIR HOME WOULD HE LOVE TO CHUCK OUT MOST?** The "cottagey" cabinet we keep our glasses and serving dishes in is something I would definitely chuck out - Camilla loves it and I hate it! • **ONE WORD HE'D USE TO SUM UP HIS LIFE...** Fantastic!

PROFILING CAMILLA

• **SIGN...** Virgo. • **LOVES...** Exercise, the beach and swimming, Russ and my family, and of course anything to do with food. • **HATES...** Laziness and mess. • **WHERE SHE GOES TO ESCAPE...** For a walk on the promenade in Cape Town to look at the sea. • **WHAT HER HOBBIES/PASSIONS ARE...** Painting, swimming, boxing, knitting and cooking for our friends. I also get it in my head to cook something that I'm determined to perfect. • **WHAT MEAL SHE'D SERVE A VISITOR IN SA...** Slow roasted oxtail served with turmeric rice, baby carrots and peas, and for dessert, flambé Crepes Suzette. • **HOW THEY REALLY, REALLY SPOIL THEMSELVES...** Go on an adventurous beach holiday with lots of sun, sea, sand and G&T's. • **WHAT SINGLE THING IN THEIR HOME WOULD SHE LOVE TO CHUCK OUT MOST?** The shelf in the lounge/TV room that keeps all Russ's crap. • **ONE WORD SHE'D USE TO SUM UP HER LIFE...** Eclectic.

ever wonder about those people who spend $2 apiece on those little bottles of Evian water?
try spelling Evian backward.

GEORGE CARLIN

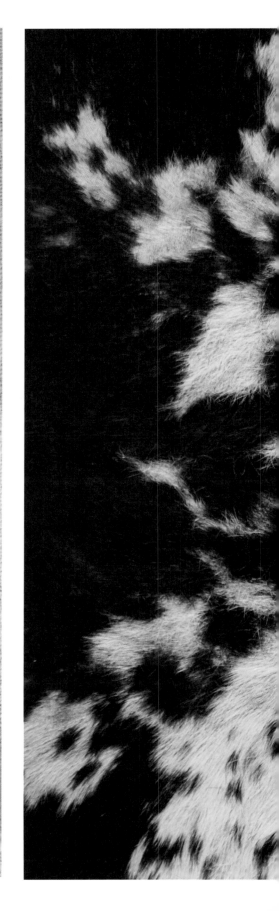

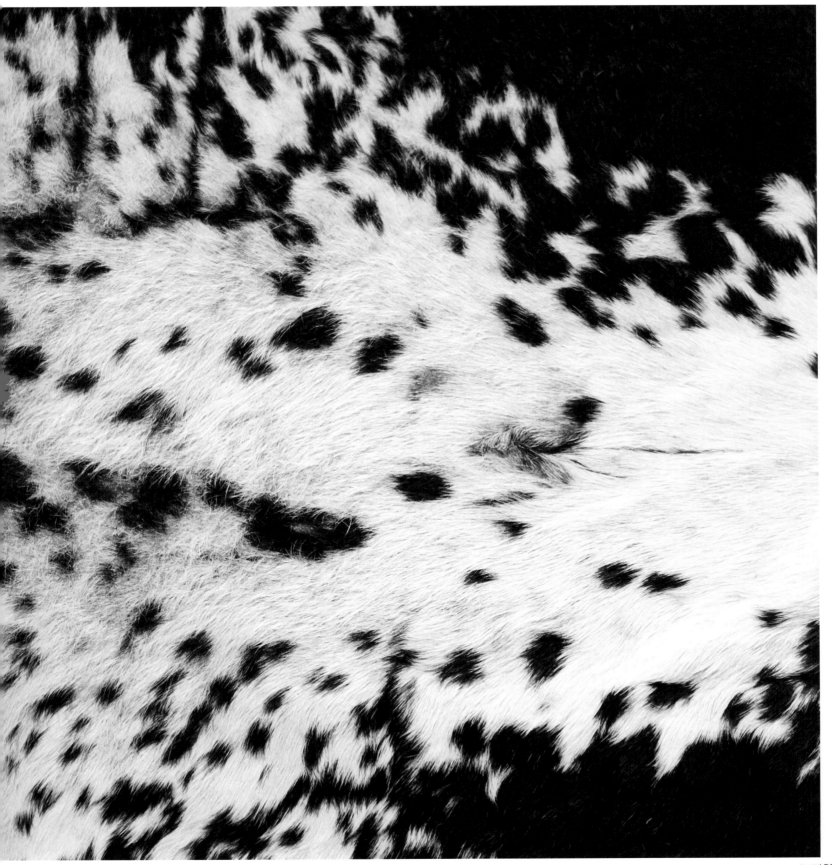

MENU
olivieh salad (Iranian chicken salad)
naan barbari (Iranian bread)
must-o-khiar with raisins & mint
lubia chiti (beans with tomato sauce)
karrysild (curried herring)
frikadeller (Danish meatballs)

Alex AND Jeannette

MELVILLE → JhB JOZI

MEET ALEXANDER MALT AND HIS VIVACIOUS WIFE, JEANNETTE MALT SORENSEN, AND STEP INSIDE THEIR JOZI HOME. I WAS VISITING JOBURG FOR THE WEEKEND AND ALONG CAME THIS INVITE FROM MY MATE BRAD, TO AN IRANIAN LUNCH. I WAS INTRIGUED… I'D NEVER MET ANYONE PERSIAN BEFORE, LET ALONE EATEN IRANIAN CUISINE.

The exotic twist? Alex (the Iranian) is married to Jeannette (the Dane) who welcomed me into their Melville home with a smiling "Salaam" followed by a swift shot of schnapps. Then we settled into 9 hours of feasting as Alex's mother, Mitra Kyai, and father, Houshang Maaghoul (visiting from Copenhagen, where they have settled), led the kitchen brigade. It was easily the longest evening feast session I've experienced, and a fine intro to the Iranian kitchen.

I had to go back for more… this time for a taste from the Iranian/Danish kitchen at lunch. Danish flavours aren't for sissies… it's pickled fish and raw onion on dense rye bread, and then sublime frikadeller with rémoulade sauce, specially brought over by visiting friends and relatives. Their fridge houses Carlsberg beer and Danish vodka. A reminder that as much as Alex and Jeannette love their new life in South Africa, they have not forgotten their roots, which are embedded in their cuisine (and booze!).

Alex found his way to SA as a representative in the cement industry. Along the way they found their lovely Melville home and started massive renovation projects. And as most people involved with building or renovations know, it's never plain sailing. Alex explains, "Here everything is hectic. We are still renovating, now two new rooms… one upstairs, one downstairs! This place is never-ending, but NO MORE! I'm so sick of workers now!" I think he needs another schnapps or two…

1. MIRANDA DU TOIT'S "WASTE ART" 2. EISH! DOWNTOWN JOZI FROM THEIR BALCONY 3. GREAT GATSBY! WHAT GLAM GLOVES JEANNETTE 4. JEANNETTE'S EMERGENCY EVACUATION PLAN 5. ALEX'S SPECIAL COLLECTION OF VERY OLD TILES FROM IRAN 6. REAL DANISH SNAPS (SCHNAPPS). IT'S GOOD, JA?! 7. 60'S STYLE PLASTIC PEARL PURSE FROM MIAMI 8. HAPPY MEMORIES OF TRAVELLING, FAMILY & FRIENDS 9. COOKBOOK INHERITED FROM JEANNETTE'S GRANDMOTHER 10. ALL THE WAY FROM DENMARK 11. ALL THINGS BRIGHT & BEAUTIFUL 12. THIS PAIR LIKE TO LIE LOW IN WINTER 13. ANTIQUE SALT & PEPPER SHAKER FROM DENMARK 14. JEANNETTE'S RETRO LOOK 15. OIL PAINTING GIVEN TO THEM BY NEIL 16. MASK FROM NEW YEARS EVE IN CAPE TOWN. *For captions relevant to other pictures in this chapter, please refer to the Addendum.*

OLIVIEH SALAD

(Iranian chicken salad)

Olivieh salad is a classic Iranian cold dish ideal for picnics, parties and lunches. In essence it is the Iranian version of a Russian salad with chopped potatoes, chicken, mayo and gherkins. Alex made this dish as a child with his mom and dad… and always ended up licking the bowl. You can also add peas if you please…

1½kg chicken breasts • 2kg potatoes • 10 eggs • 30 cornichons (tiny gherkins), chopped • 3T mayonnaise • juice of 2 lemons • salt and pepper to taste

Poach the chicken until tender. Cool and shred with a fork. Boil potatoes until tender (they should just pierce with a knife). Hard-boil the eggs. Mash the eggs and the potatoes with a fork into a rough paste. Mix with the chicken, mayo, lemon juice and cornichons. Season to taste and refrigerate. (Alex says it's great to make a big portion and eat it over the next couple of days for breakfast, lunch or dinner!)

SERVES 6

LISTEN UP

A GREAT IRANIAN ACCOMPANIMENT IS TO SERVE THIS WITH A PLATE OF SABZI (A MIXTURE OF FRESH HERBS, SUCH AS MINT, WATERCRESS, DILL AND BASIL) AND SOME CUBED FETA.

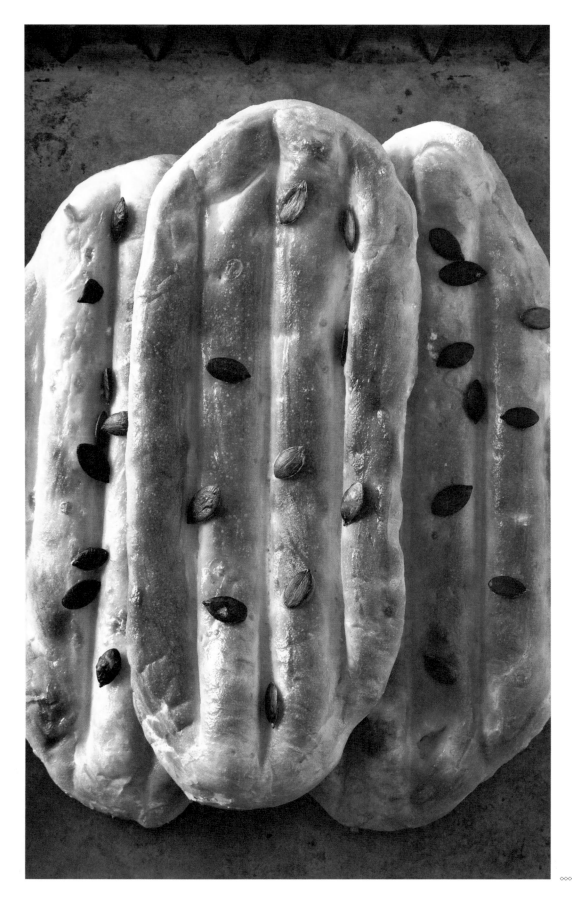

NAAN BARBARI
(Iranian bread)

Alex says that traditionally in Iran, unless you live in the mountains, you don't make your own bread… you buy it from your local baker. Since Alex's family left Iran, they could not get the same quality of bread abroad. So his dad started experimenting and ended up with this very easy recipe. Alex is proud… "My dad's bread is world-famous among our friends and family."

50g butter • 8 cups (2L) milk • 1pkt (10g) dried yeast • 2kg flour • 1t salt • 2 eggs • a handful of green pumpkin seeds

Melt the butter over a gentle heat. In a separate saucepan, warm the milk and yeast without boiling it. Cool the butter and pour it into the milk, adding the salt. Sieve the flour onto a clean work surface and make a well in the centre with your hands. Pour the liquid into the well and gently start working the flour and the milk mixture together. Knead the mixture together for a good 10 minutes. Roll into a ball and set aside for it to rise for roughly 30 minutes. Split the dough into even sized balls, the size of a small apple. Roll it flat and use a fork to make small holes in the bread. (See the picture, people.)

Beat the eggs well. Brush the top of each piece with the egg wash (beaten eggs) and sprinkle over the pumpkin seeds. Preheat your grill. Now this is the interesting part! This naan bread is simply grilled like toast under the grill. Watch carefully, as it only needs minutes on each side. Once cooked, this bread freezes remarkably well.

SERVES 6-8

LEGEND HAS IT THAT WHOEVER EATS THE LAST PIECE OF BREAD HAS TO KISS THE COOK…

MUST -O- KHIAR

with raisins & mint

This is just one of thousands of Iranian appetizers and is a version of Greek tzatsiki but with the Iranian additions of chopped walnuts, mint and raisins. The day Alex made it, he added loads of ice cubes to water it down and served it as a refreshing soup. Perfect for hot sunny days… like SA is blessed with.

500g natural yoghurt (preferably Greek yoghurt) • 3/4 cucumber • 2T olive oil • 2 garlic cloves • 1 cup (250ml) mint, finely shredded • 3T raisins • 1T walnuts, chopped finely • salt & pepper to taste

The yoghurt mustn't be watery. If the yoghurt has too much water, you need to drain it (use a coffee filter). Afterwards, if you find the yoghurt is too dry, you can always add some of the water back. Grate the cucumber and remove all the water by squeezing it between your hands. Press the garlic and mix the remainder of the ingredients together. Must-o-Khiar can easily be kept in a fridge until the next day, BUT BEWARE… the garlic will be much stronger in taste.

SERVES 6

NEIL SAYS

YOU CAN ALSO MAKE MUST-O-MASUR, WHICH IS BASICALLY SHALLOT (SMALL BROWN ONION) FLAVOURED YOGHURT. ANOTHER GREAT PERSIAN DIP.

LUBIA CHITI

(beans with tomato sauce)

This is a perfect standard Iranian vegetarian dish. You may think it sounds suspiciously like baked beans in tomato sauce (bean there, done that) but you're way wrong. This dish elevates your concept of beans to a whole new level. It's a meal in itself and may make you feel a bit like a student again… a rather exotic student, in Persia.

500g kidney beans • 1 large onion, chopped • 1t zardchube (turmeric) • 4T tomato purée • 2 cups (500ml) water • 2 potatoes • 4T olive oil • 1 lime, juiced • 1t salt • 1t chilli powder

The beans have to stay covered in water overnight. Fry the onions in 2T olive oil until translucent. Add the turmeric and the tomato purée and stir. Drain the water from the beans and add them to the pot, along with the 2 cups of water.
Turn the heat down and leave the dish to simmer for 30-45 minutes until it thickens. Boil and mash the potatoes. Add the mashed potatoes to the pot and mix together well.

To serve, add the rest of the olive oil, a splash of lime and the salt and chilli. These last ingredients must not be added to the dish until right before serving. Enjoy!

SERVES 4

tip from mitra:
During feasting ceremonies, Mitra makes her delicious Iranian Chelow rice which she cooks and mixes with yoghurt, lemon and saffron strands. She then cooks it in the pan until a wonderful golden crust forms on the bottom of the pan. This would be a perfect accompaniment to the Lubia Chiti.

THE USE OF BEANS HAS BEEN TRACED BACK AS FAR AS 6750 BC IN PARTS OF THE PRESENT-DAY MIDDLE EAST.

KARRYSILD

(curried herring)

This dish is perfect for a light lunch. Jeannette told me that in Denmark they usually eat it during Christmas time along with other fish dishes, followed by hot and savoury fare such as the Danish meatballs, called "frikadeller".

for the curry dressing:
3T sour cream • 1T mayonnaise • 1T cream • a little onion, chopped finely • curry & paprika powder (use ones that are not too strong, add to your own taste and do the same for salt & pepper) • a little sugar to enhance the curry flavour

Mix the sour cream, mayonnaise and cream together. Add your onion, sugar and spices and taste the dressing as you go until you have found the right balance. Add your dressing to the herring and stir carefully together. Refridgerate before use.

to serve:
6 good pieces of herring, sliced • 6 boiled eggs • dark rye bread

Serve a piece of the herring on rye bread, with boiled egg on the side and sliced onion on top. Remember to accompany the meal with Snaps (Danish schnapps) or a cold Carlsberg beer… they are an essential part of this dish!

SERVES 6

a bit about Danish lunch...
Dark, rye bread or brown, seeded bread is essential for all these Danish dishes. They eat good bread for breakfast with good cheeses, for lunch with everything from fish to salami, and even for dinner with anything hot or cold.

"NO MATTER WHERE WE ARE IN THE WORLD, OUR THOUGHTS ALWAYS GO BACK TO GOOD DANISH BREAD OF ALL SORTS."
- JEANNETTE

FRIKADELLER

(Danish meatballs)

Jeannette is a big fan of frikadeller, "There isn't a child or adult in Denmark that doesn't know or hasn't tasted Danish meatballs. We eat them in all sorts of ways and styles, traditional or with foreign spices and ingredients. You can serve frikadeller with hot or cold potato salad, with vegetables, in sandwiches with gherkins and mustard, as a snack for a party accompanied with other small dishes… you set the limits!"

500g minced pork & veal (half and half), if you are not able to get veal, use beef • 1 onion, chopped finely • 1 large egg • 50g flour • 1½ cups (375ml) milk • 50g butter for frying • freshly ground pepper & salt to taste • 1T Dijon mustard for serving

Stir the meat, salt and pepper for about a minute to get the flavours going. Then add the onion and egg and stir again. Add the milk and flour and make sure it's well blended into the rest of the mixture. Allow to settle in the fridge for about half an hour.

Try making a small meatball before you fry it all, then taste and see if you need to add more salt and pepper to your liking. Heat your pan and melt the butter - don't let it overheat. Use a tablespoon and the palm of your hand to shape your meatballs. Let them fry on a medium heat for about 8 minutes on each side until they are done. Be careful that they don't blacken. We serve frikadeller warm with fried bacon and mushrooms on rye bread, and a bit of Dijon mustard on the side…

SERVES 4

HEY GUYS!

MAKE A BIGGER PORTION AND FREEZE FOR LATER LUNCHES OR MAINS.

it's better to eat greens than throw up yellows.
- JEANNETTE

a little saffron in your food every day, makes you happier.
- ALEX

ALEX & JEANNETTE IN A NUTSHELL

• WHAT'S YOUR FIRST MEMORY OF SOUTH AFRICA?
The drive on the highway from Joburg Airport to Melville with our new life in SA ahead of us.

• WHAT DO YOU ALWAYS HAVE IN THE FRIDGE?
Milk and chilli sauce.

• WHERE'S YOUR NEXT SA HOLIDAY?
Knysna in April for champagne, good company and oysters.

• WHAT ARE YOUR HOPES FOR 2010?
That the world and South Africa itself will see and learn what an amazing place this country is…

• WHERE'S YOUR FAVOURITE STRETCH OF ROAD IN SA?
The road from Johannesburg to Dwaalboom (Limpopo province) via Sun City – you get to experience lakes, mountains and unique art galleries on the way… and even see giraffes!

• WHY DON'T YOU LIVE IN CAPE TOWN OR ANYWHERE ELSE?
Because Joburg rocks!

• YOUR 3 WISHES?
Alexander: Good health, passion & loooots of sex with my wife!! Oh, and to also be economically independent.

Jeannette: That one day I will get struck by fitness-mania; for family and friends to stay well; and to always have my independence.

we should
look for
someone to
eat and drink
with before
looking for
something to
eat and drink.

EPICURUS

MENU

spanspek gazpacho with ham-wrapped grissini
pastry 'pizza' with caramelised onion & taleggio
three-pork burgers wih the world's best coleslaw
Bev's glazed gammon cooked in ginger beer
granadilla tart

Kate

I ♥ CT

Tamboerskloof

KATE WILSON IS A FOODIE IN THE TRUE SENSE. GET US AROUND A TABLE TOGETHER WITH A GLASS OF WINE AND THE TALK IS ALL ABOUT FOOD, RESTAURANTS, CHEFS, SEASONAL INGREDIENTS AND TRIPS TO FAR-FLUNG FOOD HAUNTS LIKE THE *FRENCH LAUNDRY* IN CALIFORNIA. KATE HAS BEEN ON MORE FOOD PILGRIMAGES THAN MOST PEOPLE COULD EVEN DREAM OF...

Not that Kate is simply food-obsessed. She made her name in the magazine trade, as editor of *SL* magazine, then moved on to become editor of the award-winning *House and Leisure*, and is now editor of *Marie Claire* magazine. She cooks for her own pleasure and that of well-chosen guests. When it comes to supper parties, this dinner diva has an unbeaten track record.

Strangely, Kate was not a food fanatic as a child. Luckily, her mother managed to pass her love of entertaining on to her and now there are few things she enjoys more than having a dinner party. "But no matter how carefully I plan them, they never seem as magical as hers..." says Kate. "This might be because I tend to choose recipes better left to Michelin-starred chefs with science degrees... and then get horribly anxious and drink too much before cooking them." Fortunately for Kate, all her closest friends are people who love food. She doesn't think this is a conscious process... those who love to eat are naturally better people and therefore easy to love. This is important because it means they are willing to suffer her experiments and midnight servings and still come for dinner. So these are a few of Kate's favourite recipes designed for special occasions, because some people are more deserving than others...

"There is nothing more infuriating than spending several hundred Rands to home-cure salmon gravlax, only to have some Philistine whinge that they don't eat raw fish. I'm not really in the food industry, so cooking is for my pleasure, as much as for those I am feeding. Every chef I have ever interviewed has told me... they do what they do, because they like to see people happy. That's noble enough for me." Thanks, Kate!

1. CHINA TEA SET INHERITED FROM KATE'S PARENTS 2. CERAMIC SCULPTURE BY FRANK VAN REENAN 3. NOSTALGIC FIGURINE FROM KATE'S DAD 4. THE SMALL MAKINGS OF SOMETHING GREAT! 5. KATE'S PERFUME FACTORY... I MEAN, COLLECTION 6. PART OF KATE'S ELABORATE & ELITE MENU COLLECTION 7. BIRTHDAY GIFT OF FRIDA KAHLO COASTERS FROM CAZZIE 8. HER FAVOURITE CUSHION COVER BY HEATHER MOORE 9. GEMMA ORKIN CERAMIC BOWL 10. TALEGGIO CHEESE - YUM! 11. THE WORLD'S BEST GIN (& KATE'S TOO) 12. SPECIAL VILLEROY & BOCH DINNER SERVICE FROM KATE'S MOM 13. NIGELLA LAWSON LEMON SQUEEZER - "OOOH, MMM, AAAH..." 14. BIRTHDAY PRESENT FROM KATE'S STEPMOTHER 15. ORGANIC VEG FROM MILLSTONE AT THE ECO VILLAGE *OUDE MOULEN* 16. KATE'S WEEKDAY DINNER SPOT WHERE SHE WATCHES THE LATEST EPISODES OF *HOUSE*. *For captions relevant to other pictures in this chapter, please refer to the Addendum.*

SPANSPEK GAZPACHO

with ham-wrapped grissini

This is Kate's best foodie friend, Nikki Werner's recipe, inspired by an issue of *Gourmet Traveller*. Kate and Nikki have enjoyed some of their most memorable meals together. They also joke about being part of the famous Team *El Bulli* – they ate there in 2005. Nikki served this meal at a combined family Christmas. The main course was Turducken (turkey stuffed with a duck, stuffed with a chicken), but this was the highlight. It's rather like a deconstructed version of the classic Parma ham and melon starter, with the ham served on the side.

for the gazpacho:
50g ciabatta, crusts removed • 100g blanched almonds, chopped roughly • 4 garlic cloves, chopped roughly • 1/3 cup (80ml) extra virgin olive oil • 2T sherry vinegar • 2 cups (500ml) cold water • ¾ of a spanspek, peeled, seeded and chopped • sea salt flakes and freshly ground pepper to season • verjuice for seasoning (optional)

to serve:
sea salt flakes and freshly ground black pepper to season • Borges fried garlic olive oil • bocconcini mozzarella balls (optional) • Black Forest or Parma ham • bread or grissini (bread sticks)

Put the bread into a shallow bowl of water to soak. Put the almonds in a food processor and pulse until they are roughly chopped. Add the garlic and process until the mixture is very finely chopped. Remove the bread from the water, squeeze dry and add to the food processor. Also add the olive oil, sherry vinegar, water and spanspek and process until smooth. Season to taste (add more sherry vinegar if necessary or a dash of verjuice to balance the flavours), then serve with more sea salt flakes, ground pepper and a generous drizzle of the garlic olive oil. Float a few balls of bocconcini (3-4 per bowl) in the soup. Serve with Black Forest ham and bread, or with the ham wrapped around breadsticks on the side.

MAKES ABOUT 1¼L - SERVES 6

PASTRY 'PIZZA'
with caramelised onion & taleggio

This is a Nigel Slater recipe from his book *Appetite* that Kate's friend, Catherine, has been making for years (it's great stomach-lining finger food for drinks parties and as a starter at dinners and braais). Nigel is probably Kate's favourite food writer of all time. His recipes are all about making one or two ingredients shine - like a pan of sticky golden onions browning in a pool of butter married with ripe, oozing cheese. Total food porn. You can make this with red onions and Parmesan, or with brie instead of taleggio and it looks incredibly impressive, but is so simple.

6 medium onions • 50g butter
• 200g (one roll) puff pastry
• 129g taleggio • 1t thyme leaves

Preheat the oven to 220°C. Peel the onions and cut them in half, then into thick wedges. Melt the butter in a shallow pan and fry the onions on a low heat, very slowly, so that they caramelise (this is crucial and will take at least 20 minutes). Roll out the pastry and put it on a floured baking sheet. Draw a square about 2cm from the edge of the pastry and spoon the onions into this area.

Cut the cheese into slices, then tear into bits and tuck in among the onions. Sprinkle with the thyme leaves and season. Brush the exposed edges of the pastry with melted butter from the onions. Put it in the oven for 20 minutes or until the pastry is puffed and the onions are golden. Turn the grill on for a minute if you want the onions to char slightly. Cut into wedges and serve in napkins.

SERVES 4

P.S. You can also make individual 'pies' as we did for this shoot.

"ALMOST ANYTHING IS EDIBLE WITH A DAB OF FRENCH MUSTARD ON IT." - NIGEL SLATER

Paul Smith

THREE-PORK BURGERS

with the world's best coleslaw

This recipe is inspired by *Lucques'* Suzanne Goin. Kate simplified it and left out the cheese in the interest of her guests' survival. Three kinds of pork and garlic mayo is enough of a cholesterol challenge without a slab of cheddar. She made these for a summer braai, with homemade coleslaw, which her mother said was the best she'd ever eaten.

for the patties:
1½t cumin seeds • 3T olive oil
• ½ cup (125ml) shallots, diced
• 1T garlic, chopped • 1T thyme leaves
• 2 mild green chillies, sliced • 1¾t salt
& some black pepper • 1kg pork mince
• 100g smoked back bacon, diced
• 100g chorizo, without skin
• 2T flat-leaf parsley

for serving:
burger buns • garlic mayonnaise (aioli)
• rocket leaves • coleslaw

Toast the cumin seeds in a dry pan over a medium heat until they darken slightly and start to smell aromatic. Grind in a pestle and mortar. Return pan to a high heat, add olive oil and shallots, turn heat down and cook for a few minutes until the onions soften. Add the garlic, thyme, cumin and chillies. Season with ¼t salt and some black pepper and continue to cook until the onions become translucent. Leave to cool. Put the minced pork, chorizo, bacon, cooled shallot mixture and parsley in a mixing bowl and use your hands to combine. Don't over-mix the meat. Season with 1½t salt and black pepper. Shape into patties that will fit your burger buns (about 170g each) and put them in the fridge to firm up. Allow the patties to come to room temperature before brushing each with olive oil and grilling, either on the braai when coals are not too hot, or on a grill pan. Grill for 3-4 minutes and then turn over and cook for another 3 minutes - do not overcook. (They SHOULD still be pink in the centre or they won't be juicy.) Slice the buns in half, brush with olive oil and toast on the grill or braai, cut-side down. Spread the burger buns with aioli, top with some rocket, a burger patty and a helping of coleslaw.

FOR THE COLESLAW RECIPE, PLEASE REFER TO THE ADDENDUM
SERVES 6

BEV'S GLAZED GAMMON

cooked in ginger beer

Kate's aunt Beverley, a "nose-to-tail" gourmet, makes the juiciest gammon. This is her recipe. Kate usually makes it for Christmas Eve dinner at her Dad's. She says, "When I arrive with the huge covered platter, his eyes literally light up." You could eat this dish hot, but really, it's summer in SA, hey? Frankly, it's MUCH better boiled the day before, roasted in the morning and eaten cold with a sweet onion salad.

for the gammon:
5kg smoked gammon, uncooked & on the bone • 4L ginger beer • 1t peppercorns • a handful of dry mustard powder • 1 cup (250ml) of brown sugar • 1T cloves

for the basting:
1 cup (250ml) pineapple fruit juice • 1 cup (250ml) honey • 5ml fine ginger • 5ml mustard powder • 1-2 tins (880g) pineapple rings

The day before dinner, put the gammon into the biggest pot you can find with the ginger beer and peppercorns, and bring to the boil. Boil for 25 minutes per 500g. Leave to cool in the liquid. Remove the gammon from the pot and peel off the brown rind, leaving the fat behind... there should be a thick layer of fat all over the meat. When cool, score the fat all over in criss-cross diamond shapes. Now dredge the gammon very liberally in dry mustard and brown sugar. Rub lots of both into the scored fat and pat it in firmly. It should completely cover the meat. Stud each diamond with a clove. Leave the gammon in the fridge overnight.

The next day preheat the oven to 200°C and combine all the basting ingredients in a small saucepan on the stove. (If you are serving this cold in the afternoon, do this in the morning, otherwise do it just before your guests arrive.) Roast the gammon in a hot oven for 20-30 minutes, basting every five minutes with the syrup. After 20 minutes, dredge the meat again with more sugar and mustard and continue to baste for a final 20 minutes. Watch closely, don't let it get too dark.

Lower the heat to 180°C and cook without basting for another 20 minutes. If you are serving the gammon hot, it can be removed and carved now, against the grain. If you are serving it cold, remove from the oven and cool. Using toothpicks, cover the surface of the gammon with pineapple rings – very retro. Carve when you are ready to serve.

SERVES 8

L-R: 1. KATE'S RECIPE BOOK COLLECTION 2. VIVIENNE WESTWOOD SHOES, MADE ENTIRELY OF RUBBER 3. DAVID HOCKNEY PORTRAIT OF CELIA BIRTWELL 4. KATE'S GROCERY BAG FROM HER FRIEND, POLLY 5. KATE IMPERSONATING NIGELLA LAWSON… OR IS IT VICE VERSA?! 6. ONE OF KATE'S TWO BELOVED CATS, FRANNY *OPPOSITE:* GIFT FROM BIRDS CAFÉ IN CAPE TOWN

Thinking
of
Bricklane.
o/*

GRANADILLA TART

Kate's been making this for years and her sweet-toothed sister always begs her to do it when she is coming for dinner. She often makes it when there are children around… so they can see the blowtorching bit and crack their piece with a spoon.

250g short-crust pastry • 250g castor sugar • 4 eggs • 1 cup (250ml) cream • 200ml granadilla pulp • 2T lemon juice • brown sugar to top • cream to serve

Preheat the oven to 180°C. Press the pastry into a tart tin (preferably springform) and blind bake using the greaseproof paper and weights method (read the tip below). For the filling, put the castor sugar, eggs, cream, granadilla pulp and lemon juice into a bowl and whisk to combine. Pour the filling into the pastry case and bake for 30 minutes or until the filling is just set. It'll come out a bit wobbly and will firm up in the fridge. When ready to serve, sprinkle the tart with the brown sugar and place under a hot grill for a few seconds or use a blowtorch to caramelise the sugar. Serve with whipped cream.

tip from kate:

BLIND BAKING… Press the pastry into a springform tart tin. Prick the pastry all over with a fork, then put a piece of greaseproof paper, (cut into a circle) into the tin (covering the pastry). Use two handfuls of baking weights, rice or dry beans, to weigh the paper down. Put in the oven at 180°C for 15 minutes. Take out the oven and remove the paper and the weights and bake for a further 5 minutes until the pastry case is nicely browned. Set aside to cool.

SERVES 8

KATE SAYS

"I LIKE TO THINK I'M ENCOURAGING THE NEXT GENERATION'S APPRECIATION OF FOOD."

THE LOW DOWN ON KATE...

I LOVE early mornings on bush holidays. The view from my terrace over the Tamboerskloof rooftops in the late afternoon and the view of Table Mountain from my office. Team *El Bulli*: my best foodie friends Nikki and Polly who ate there with me a few years ago – it was an unforgettable trip. My crazy, neurotic, character-filled family and the very few occasions we are all together at once.

I DO NOT LOVE deadlines. Or meetings. Travelling economy class. People who don't dress up for dinner or the theatre.

MY FAVOURITE PLACE IN THE WORLD is *La Boqueria* market in Barcelona where pure happiness is a plate of grilled sardines and a glass of chilled Cava at *Bar Pinotxo*.

WHAT I WOULD MISS MOST ABOUT SA is my family. When I lived in London I sometimes felt real, physical pain being away from my parents and siblings. It was too hard to stand, so I came home.

OF ALL THE PLACES IN SA I COULD LIVE I chose Cape Town as it's small enough to feel like a village and cosmopolitan enough to still be interesting and envied by the rest of the world.

MY HOBBIES AND PASSIONS include food, travel, storytelling and nostalgia (if that can be a passion). My favourite thing in the world is to plan a trip somewhere new, then buy travel guides, research the local scene and make lists of things to do and eat. I'm also very sentimental and I love stories, so I struggle to get rid of things that have memories attached to them. I've even kept a letter my sister, Romy, wrote to me when I moved to London. It was in an envelope with the following address: Katie Wilson, Jamie Oliver's House, London. She was 15 at the time.

MY PASSIONS HAVE enhanced my home... I collect cookbooks, kitchenware and ceramics, mostly because I always imagine what they will look like with food in them. I also have a collection of prints and postcards from all the art galleries I've visited, and menus from all the restaurants I've eaten at around the world. I also love the things I have been given that belong in my family and which I want to pass on: China teacups and a lily-patterned Villeroy & Boch dinner service my mother gave me; my grandmother's Royal Doulton Beatrix Potter figurines; a brass carriage clock from my dad's family.

HOME TASTES LIKE roast chicken and sticky roast potatoes, and the cupcakes that Patricia, our domestic worker, baked when we were children.

ONE WORD I'D USE TO SUM UP MY LIFE IS... Full.

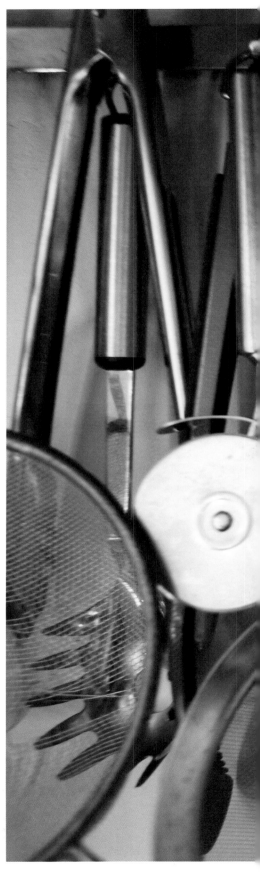

eating rice cakes
is like chewing on
a foam coffee cup,
only less filling.

DAVE BARRY

MENU

North African mezze spread
red pepper & preserved lemon salad
spiced labneh balls
Moroccan vegetable stew
harissa
slow roasted lamb
rose-petal poached pears & pistachio nut brittle
halva ice-cream
honey phyllo pastry biscuits

Rowan Ruth AND Sophie

UMHLANGA DURBAN

A LIFETIME OF BUSINESS AND PLEASURE TRAVEL. THAT'S BASICALLY WHAT'S SHAPED RUTH AND RO'S LIFE… AND WHO SAYS THERE'S ANYTHING WRONG WITH DIPPING IN AND OUT OF INTERNATIONAL LIFESTYLES? THE FACT THAT THEY CHOOSE TO WORK AND LIVE IN DURBAN, SOUTH AFRICA, SAYS A LOT ABOUT THE LIFESTYLE THAT OUR COUNTRY HAS TO OFFER.

Besides, if they chose to live anywhere else, what would I do without my lively phone chats with Ruth and spontaneous visits to their home. Their door is always open and the generous way they welcome my kids and I is always heartfelt. Their new home is a culmination of years of work, and the fact that they prefer to find themselves here on the weekends, as opposed to flitting off, is testament to the beauty of the bolt-hole that Ruth has designed. Ruth trained as a clothing designer and now finds herself dedicated to one of the most charming little girls I've ever met, her daughter, Sophie Duke. Having got to know Ruthie over the last 5 years or so, I've discovered that the woman has too much energy to be stopped… she writes a column on design trend for *Condé Nast House and Garden* and dips her fingers into various successful retail ventures. When it comes to food, Ruth can just as easily whip up a tapas plate for 4 or style up a glamorous full-on, sit-down 4-course meal for 10 without even flinching.

Rowan has found himself in some of the world's most reputable dining establishments (*Nobu HK*, *Spoon*, Gordon Ramsay's *Maze* in London), but can just as happily eat steamed dim sum at the local Chinese restaurant down a side street in Hong Kong, as enoy a casual lunch at *Sailors Thai* in Sydney. In fact, if I sniff out something new, Ro and Ruth will make a mini pilgrimage to find the spot, and vice versa. I guess we are food lovers united in friendship.

Ruth and Rowan wouldn't dream of going to Paris and not eating at *Chez Omar* in the 3rd arrondissement. They specialise in Moroccan and Algerian food and do one particular lamb dish that has visitors and local Parisians going back, over and over again. *Chez Omar* has a signature dish, which is a 'wet' couscous preparation, as opposed to the more commonly known Moroccan dry couscous dishes, like tagines. Waiters bring bowls of light couscous, a vegetable stew, slow-cooked lamb and harissa. You scoop some couscous into a bowl and add some bits of lamb, then spoon over the veggie stew. Season with the harissa and it's absolutely one of the best things one can taste. It's a great meal to serve a crowd as it's all prep that can be done way beforehand for unfussy entertaining. And it's interactive with all that bowl-passing that will be going on. What ya waiting for?!

1. LITTLE SOPHIE LOVES TO MAKE A SPLASH 2. ANTHONY SHAPIRO VASE 3. WOODCUT BY SANDY MARITZ 4. ROWAN'S SISTER'S ROTRING PEN ON PAPER DRAWING 5. A GIFT BY LYNN RUSSEL HANGING IN SOPHIE'S ROOM 6. SOPHIE'S TEENY AUSTRALIAN *CONVERSE* 7. RUTH & RO'S BEDROOM 8. BOOKEND GIVEN BY A FRIEND YEARS AGO 9. SNACKS WITH A BIT MORE BITE! 10. SOPHIE'S FAVOURITE SLEEPING TOY 11. RUTH'S YARN-DYED CORDUROY OTTOMAN IN HER DRESSING ROOM 12. VINTAGE SILVER TEA SET 13. WATER GLASSES FROM A COLOURFUL COLLECTION 14. KELLY HOPPEN GLASSES GIVEN FOR RUTH'S 40TH BIRTHDAY 15. BEAUTIFUL BOWL GIVEN TO RUTH BY HER FRIEND, ANGIE 16. CLOSE UP OF THERESA-ANNE MACKINTOSH PAINTING. *For captions relevant to other pictures in this chapter, please refer to the Addendum.*

NORTH AFRICAN MEZZE SPREAD

pine nut stuffed kibbeh:
200g bulgar wheat • 350g lamb or beef mince • 1 onion, grated • 1t cinnamon • 1t nutmeg • 1t salt • 1t pepper • 100g pine nuts

Soak the bulgar wheat in hot water for about 15 minutes until it's hydrated. Mix with all the above ingredients. Roll a golf ball-sized mixture around your middle finger to form a cavity. Remove finger and fill the hole with a teaspoon of pine nuts. Seal the ends, making sure there are no cracks. Fry in batches in 5cm of oil until golden brown. Drain and serve with the red pepper & yoghurt dipping sauce.

FOR THE RED PEPPER & YOGHURT DIP RECIPE, PLEASE REFER TO THE ADDENDUM

pickled turnips:
500g turnips (medium-sized, quartered) • ½ raw beetroot, peeled and sliced • a few red chillies • 200ml red wine vinegar • 2 cups (500ml) water • ½t allspice • ½t black peppercorns • 3T salt • 4 garlic cloves

Heat together the vinegar, water, allspice, peppercorns and salt for a few minutes. Season with more salt if necessary. Arrange the veg in a sterilised jar and pour the completely cool liquids over them. Seal and leave in the fridge for 7-10 days. Serve the beetroot wedges in a dish with chillies and black olives.

mini flatbreads:
100ml warm water • ¼t dried yeast • 130g unbleached flour • ¼t salt • 1T olive oil

Stir the yeast into the water. Place the flour and salt in a bowl. Start at the side of the bowl, pouring in a little of the yeast-water and incorporating the flour into it little by little. Then beat in the olive oil. Knead the dough, making sure there are no lumps. Leave to stand for 20 minutes. Knead a little more. Flour a surface, and your hands, and shape into a golf ball-sized piece of dough. Then pat down into a circle and roll into an elongated flatbread with a rolling pin. Heat up a frying pan over medium heat and fry the flatbread. When it starts to bubble, turn it over. It's done when both sides are covered in brown bubbles. The bread should be thin but pliable.

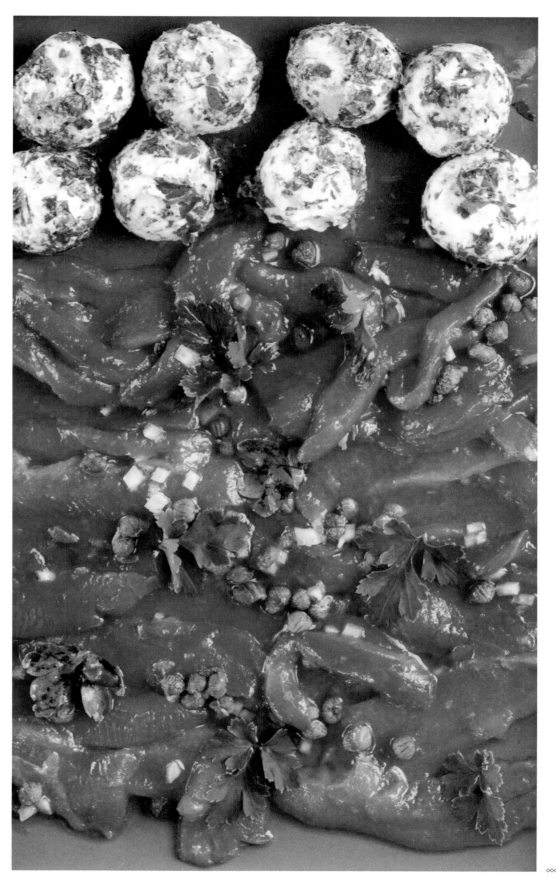

RED PEPPER & PRESERVED LEMON SALAD

Making your own preserved lemons is a doddle. Simply slice a lemon into quarters, but not all the way through. Then stuff loads of rock salt in between the wedges. Cram it into a preserving jar and top up with freshly squeezed lemon juice. In 4-6 weeks the rind should have softened and become well "pickled". It's fantastic mixed into mayo as a dip, used in an olive tapenade or, as in this recipe, sprinkled over char-grilled peppers.

4 large red bell peppers, deseeded, grilled, & peeled • rind of ½ a preserved lemon, sliced finely with pith removed • 1 garlic clove, chopped • 3T olive oil • a squeeze of lemon • black pepper to taste • 50g capers, rinsed • 2T parsley, chopped roughly

Tear the peppers into long strips and place in a bowl with the olive oil, lemon juice and sliced zest, pepper and garlic. Toss to coat. It should not need any salt because of the salty capers and preserved lemon. Arrange on a plate with the capers and parsley sprinkled on top.

a great accompaniment:
spiced labneh balls
12 labneh balls • 2t fenugreek seeds • ½t cumin seeds • 1 dried chilli • olive oil to taste • salt & pepper to taste

Buy labneh balls and halve and re-roll into smaller balls. Crush in a mortar with a pestle, 2t of fenugreek seeds, ½t cumin seeds and 1 dried chilli. Add a little olive oil and black pepper (check for salt and add if you choose). Roll the labneh balls in this mixture.

also serve with:
good green olives • grilled slices of chorizo sausage (Woolworths do a brilliant Spanish chorizo)

SERVES 6

ALL MAMMALS CAN TASTE THE BURNING SENSATION OF PEPPER. BIRDS, HOWEVER, CAN'T!

L-R: 1. MAIN BATHROOM WITH OS-SHUTTER CONCRETE CARRARA MARBLE 2. OUTSIDE VERANDAH WHERE RUTH & ROWAN ENJOY ENTERTAINING 3. HG CHAIR BY TONIC DESIGN 4. WEDDING GIFTS & 40TH BIRTHDAY PRESENTS FROM FRIENDS 5. SOPHIE'S CHEERFUL BEDROOM 6. ANCESTRAL PICTURE RUTH INHERITED FROM HER MOTHER'S SIDE OF THE FAMILY *OPPOSITE:* THIS PICTURE IS PRICELESS!

MOROCCAN VEGETABLE STEW

Although I haven't eaten at *Chez Omar*, I have eaten at similar Arab haunts in Paris and can vouch for this style of eating... I ordered an additional side of char-grilled chilli peppers as well as extra harissa – just to spice up the whole lot even more...

1 onion, chopped finely • 1T olive oil • ½t turmeric • ¼t cayenne pepper • 1 cinnamon stick • 3 cloves • 1½t black pepper • ½t salt • 4 cups (1L) vegetable stock • 1 tin (65g) tomato paste • 4 medium carrots, cut into 2cm chunks • 4 medium zucchinis, cut into 2cm chunks • 1 tin (400g) chickpeas

In a pot, over medium heat, sautée the onion in the oil until translucent. Add the spices, cinnamon stick and seasoning and fry for a minute or so. Add the stock and tomato paste and bring to the boil. Add the carrots and zucchini and reduce heat to a simmer. Simmer for about half an hour until vegetables are cooked. Add chickpeas at the end and make sure they are heated through. Ladle into a serving bowl.

SERVES 6

for the couscous:
1 box (500g) couscous • coriander, chopped lightly

Prepare as per instructions on box. Arrange cooked, fluffy couscous in a bowl and sprinkle with a little roughly chopped coriander.

FOR THE HARISSA PASTE RECIPE, PLEASE REFER TO THE ADDENDUM

THE MESMERISING NATURAL SPLENDOUR OF MOROCCO HAS WON IT THE NAME OF THE 'OASIS OF THE SENSES'.

SLOW ROASTED LAMB

When this lamb dish arrived out of the oven, it was so tender it just fell apart... that's what slow cooking is all about.

• **approximately 2kg leg of lamb, on the bone • juice of 2 lemons • 8-10 garlic cloves • salt & pepper • 60g butter • 50ml olive oil • 1 cup (250ml) water**

Preheat oven to 220℃. Wash the leg of lamb and pat dry. Place in a large baking dish. Slash through skin and fat with a big serrated knife in diagonal stripes about 2cm apart, across the joint. Rub lemon juice onto the meat and pour the remaining juice into a baking dish. Peel the garlic, halve it lengthwise and insert into the incisions. Season with salt and pepper and dot the meat with the butter.

Pour the olive oil and water around the meat, into the baking dish. Bake for 20 minutes uncovered to brown the meat. Turn the lamb over and brown the other side at the same temperature. Reduce heat to 150℃, cover with foil and bake for 4-5 hours, turning every hour, until the meat is crisp on the outside and really tender on the inside.

SERVES 6

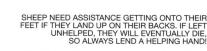

SHEEP NEED ASSISTANCE GETTING ONTO THEIR FEET IF THEY LAND UP ON THEIR BACKS. IF LEFT UNHELPED, THEY WILL EVENTUALLY DIE, SO ALWAYS LEND A HELPING HAND!

ROSE-PETAL POACHED PEARS

with pistachio nut brittle

for the rose-petal poached pears:
2/3 cup of sugar • a few pieces of lemon zest (cut into 2 x 4cm pieces) • 1 cinnamon stick • 4 small ripe pears, peeled with the stalks left on • 2 red roses, organic and untreated (petals only) • 1t rose water • 2 cups (500ml) water

To make the pears, boil all the ingredients (except the pears) for 5 minutes to infuse the flavours. Add the pears and simmer gently for about 15 minutes until cooked. Remove pears and set aside.

Reduce the liquid until it makes a thin syrup. Strain and reserve the syrup.

for the pistachio nut brittle:
50g pistachio nuts, unshelled & unsalted • 3T sugar

Oil a tray and arrange the nuts in little strips. Place sugar in a pan and heat over medium heat for about 4 minutes until you have a caramel. Remember to swirl the pan to move the caramel around and not stir. Pour caramel over the nuts and leave to set.

SERVES 6

a great accompaniment: halva ice-cream

I am a huge fan of jazzing-up good vanilla ice cream with all sorts of additions. In this case, I would take a tub of good vanilla ice-cream and leave it out of the fridge until it's a bit soft. Crumble a big halva bar into small and large chunks into a bowl. Add the ice-cream and mix through. Refreeze once mixed.

PEARS RIPEN FROM THE INSIDE OUT. TO SPEEDEN UP RIPENING, PLACE THEM NEXT TO BANANAS IN A FRUIT BOWL. THEY'LL STAY FRESH FOR LONGER IF KEPT IN A FRIDGE.

HONEY PHYLLO PASTRY BISCUITS

for the phyllo pastry biscuits:
4 sheets of phyllo pastry • 50g melted
butter • a handful of castor sugar
• 3T runny honey

Preheat oven to 180˚C. Brush a baking tray with a little butter and lay the first layer of phyllo pastry on top. Sprinkle lightly with a little sugar. Place the next layer on top and brush again, sprinkling more sugar. On the top layer, brush with melted butter and drizzle honey all over the top. Cut into long rectangular biscuits. Bake in the preheated oven for 10 mins or until golden brown.

To serve, arrange a pear and a ball of ice-cream on a plate. Sprinkle with crushed pistachio nuts, drizzle a little syrup over and serve with the pistachio nut brittle and biscuits.

SERVES 6

HONEY DATES BACK FOR 150 MILLION YEARS. IT IS WRITTEN ABOUT IN HIEROGLYPHICS AND EGYPTIANS WOULD USE IT AS A FORM OF PAYMENT, LIKE THE AZTECS USED COCOA BEANS.

watermelon - it's a good fruit. you eat, you drink, you wash your face.

- ENRICO CARUSO

ALL ABOUT ROWAN AND RUTH

• **WE'RE LOVING** flowers, travel, gardening, books and eating the greatest food • **NOT SO MUCH LOVING** being kept waiting or told 'no' • **WE FIRST HOOKED UP BECAUSE** we'd known each other forever and then there was a really great dinner at *Perrins* restaurant with too much wine! Ruth made the first move... • **COMMON INTERESTS ARE** food definitely! And travel, design and books • **IN 10 YEARS TIME** we hope we're healthy, happy and still in possession of all our family • Ricky Gervais **MAKES US LAUGH** • **WE LOVE LIFE IN DURBS BECAUSE** it's where our friends and family are, and the weather is grand all year round! • **OUR HOME SMELLS LIKE** freshly mowed lawn, leather and lemons • **WE REALLY, REALLY SPOIL OURSELVES BY** travelling the world and trying out great restaurants along the way. We get all excited about our bookings and make to-do lists, then read restaurant reviews, prioritise them and shortlist them. It's a big thing • **OUR SAFEST PLACE IN THE WORLD IS** home • **WE NORMALLY EAT** breakfast and dinner at the table but lunch can be a more casual arrangement • **WE'RE SORRY TO CONFESS THAT** we've leopard crawled past the front door to avoid unwanted visitors before. Yes, we have.

if junk food is the devil, then a sweet orange is a scripture.

AUDREY FORIS

marinated traffic light peppers
pickled octopus tapas & potato salad
marinated mushrooms with grissini
white pepper Carpaccio & homemade mayo
BBQ deboned quail with fennel skewered potatoes
zucchini rolls stuffed with ricotta
squid ink & prawn ravioli
sweet potato gnocchi with warm salsa verde
cranberry jelly & liquorice ice-cream

Greg AND Roché
drummond
KZN

GREG AND ROCHÉ ARE TRUE BLUE FRIENDS… AND BEFORE I BEGIN TO ULULATE ABOUT THEIR PROFESSIONAL ACHIEVEMENTS AND HOW PROUD I AM OF THEM, I'LL START WITH THE GLUE THAT BINDS US.

I have witnessed the birth of their children, Levi (7) and Gracie (5), who are almost cousins to my two kids; I accidently spat beer over Roché in her red wedding dress (designed by my wife, Colleen Eitzen); I've shared so many lunches at our Drummond home that kicked off at 11am and ended way past any sensible person's bedtime; and I've spent many long weekends at our beach cottage with them, where as much time is spent in the kitchen as on the beach. They are my family, my other brother and sister.

And boy oh boy can they cook. The ease with which Greg and Roché cook is a true indication of their creativity. We've gone through many food phases together (the Korean phase lasted just a tad too long). We could never get enough Italian, or Chinese, or Vietnamese Nuoc Mam sauce, and who can forget Roché's fascination with cured meats (charcuterie). One fridge in their Drummond home is like a mortuary filled with pieces of meat, slaughtered and hung. However, it was this initial experimentation that led them to a new and thriving business called *Chuck & Bobs* – a home delivery service that specialises in home-cured product, organic and sustainable produce. That's what I love most about Greg & Roché, they dream and make things happen.

Their interior design practice, *Egg Designs*, has garnered many awards. They have exhibited nationally and in New York and London, and have done interiors ranging from mass market retail, to boutique hotels (their latest being *The Concierge Boutique Bungalows* in Durban). What sets them apart is their unique ability to define a new African sensibility. One that askews tradition and blazes a trail of individual thought and comfort. After all, why would you want to live under a myriad of Nguni hides and Ndebele prints when you can rather have a real ostrich foot lamp next to your bed?! Now you see why I love them so much… Mwah!

1. WARNING: BIG & SMALL CHILDREN ALWAYS AT PLAY 2. EGG DESIGN MOTIF BY CLAIRE CLARK, ON THEIR DINING ROOM CHAIRS 3. WE STILL CAN'T GET ENOUGH OF ITALIAN FOOD 4. ANTIQUE CRYSTAL CHANDELIER 5. WARTHOG HORN TROPHY 6. SHOWER POWER! 7. A STEEL PLATE ETCHING BY BRONWYN VAUGHN EVANS 8. ONE OF THE MANY ARTWORKS HANGING IN THEIR LOUNGE 9. EGG DESIGN WALLPAPER IN THEIR MAIN BEDROOM 10. CHARCOAL DRAWING BY ANETE NORVAL 11. AGED WALL IN ROCHÉ'S VEGETABLE GARDEN 12. HAVING 2 SMALL CHILDREN CAN BE A "HARE RAISING" EXPERIENCE 13. GREG & ROCHÉ'S DRUMMOND GARDEN IN FULL SPLENDOUR 14. SKY, 1 OF GREG & ROCHÉ'S 3 DOGS 15. GABIAN STONEWALL LINKING THE INSIDE & OUTSIDE OF THE HOUSE 16. OIL PAINTING BY DEE DONALDSON. *For captions relevant to other pictures in this chapter, please refer to the Addendum.*

MARINATED TRAFFIC LIGHT PEPPERS

When Roché arrives at my house and I'm running around like a headless chicken, she always whispers sagaciously in my ear, "You should have prepped, Bob (my nickname)". The controlled Virgo in her allows her to be super-sorted in the kitchen. Everything's pre-cooked and pre-chopped so that she can enjoy a glass of wine, the company and these Antipasto dishes, all prepared well ahead of time.

2 red peppers • 2 green peppers • 2 yellow peppers • 2 green chillies, blanched • 2 garlic cloves, blanched • 1 bay leaf • a sprig of rosemary • 1T capers • 6 anchovy fillets • 100ml olive oil • 50ml red wine vinegar

Char peppers under a grill until black. Leave them in a bowl covered with cling film to steam for 10 minutes. Then remove, deseed, peel and slice. Pack the peppers, chilli, garlic, bay leaf, rosemary, capers & anchovies into a sterilized jar. Drizzle with olive oil and vinegar, making sure everything is completely covered. Store in the fridge for up to 3 months. The liquid from the jar also makes a great dressing.

SERVES 4

 HUMANS HAVE LONG BELIEVED THAT ROSEMARY CAN IMPROVE MEMORY, WHICH IS WHY IT WAS OFTEN USED IN WEDDINGS (TO HELP THE COUPLE REMEMBER THEIR VOWS) & IN FUNERALS (SO THE DEAD WOULD NOT BE FORGOTTEN).

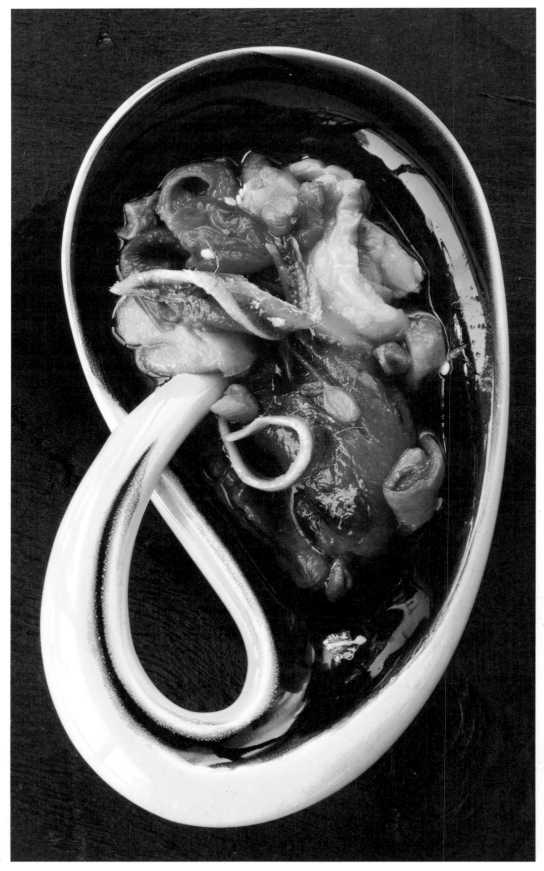

PICKLED OCTOPUS TAPAS
& potato salad

Octopus in South Africa is a little misunderstood… it seems to be a by-product of the fishing industry and sits in the freezers at fish shops calling out "PICK ME! PICK ME!". I love it and so does Roché (ok, Roché does not eat seafood but she likes to cook it). The only thing she always gets me to do is cut the head off… nice one, Shakey!

2 medium octopi (frozen)
• 2 red chillies, chopped • 1 cup parsley, chopped • 2 celery stalks • 2 garlic cloves, whole • ½ cup extra virgin olive oil • 3 potatoes, scrubbed and boiled • 2 garlic cloves, chopped • 1 red onion, chopped • a small bunch of chives, chopped • ¼ cup red wine vinegar • salt & pepper for seasoning

Clean both octopi and remove their eyes. Put 1 chilli, half the parsley, celery, 2 whole garlic cloves and ¼ cup of extra virgin olive oil into a casserole pot. Add the octopi, covering them with a lid and simmer gently for 1½ hours. Leave to cool. Boil the potatoes until tender, then drain, peel and cube. When the octopi are cooled, peel and chop them into large pieces before placing them into a serving bowl. Add 1 chilli, chopped garlic, the rest of the parsley, red onion and chives, then mix together. Then add the balance of extra virgin olive oil and red wine vinegar, with salt and pepper to taste. Before serving, dress the side potatoes with more olive oil and an additional splash of red wine vinegar, topped with salt and pepper to taste.

SERVES 10

DID YOU KNOW? AN OCTOPUS HAS 3 HEARTS & ITS BLOOD IS BRIGHT BLUE.

MARINATED MUSHROOMS

with grissini

40g porcini mushrooms, dried
• **50g butter** • **2 garlic cloves, chopped**
• **200g button mushrooms, sliced**
• **50ml red wine vinegar** • **50ml olive oil**
• **1T parsley, chopped** • **salt & pepper
to taste**

Soak the porcini mushrooms in boiling water for 20 minutes, then drain. Melt the butter in a pan until bubbling. Then add the porcini mushrooms, garlic and button mushrooms. Sweat for 20 minutes, but do not fry. Put them all into a bowl and add vinegar, olive oil and parsley. Refrigerate overnight to absorb the flavours. Before serving bring to room temperature and add salt and pepper to taste.

SERVES 4

for the grissini:
50g butter • **200g milk** • **1pkt (10g) fresh
yeast** • **375g bread flour** • **10g salt** • **3T
grated Parmesan** • **flour for dusting**

Melt butter in a pan, add the milk and heat until lukewarm. Then whisk in the yeast. Put the flour, salt and Parmesan in a bowl and gradually add the yeast mixture, mixing it with your hands until it forms a dough. Knead for 10 minutes and cover with a damp tea towel for 30 minutes. Knead for a further 5 minutes, cover with a damp tea towel and leave for another 30 minutes. Cut the dough in half. Roll out each piece, on a floured work surface, into a large rectangular shape.

Cut the dough into 1cm strips. Roll each strip with your fingertips working outwards and stretching as you roll. Press each end and lay out the dough on a floured baking sheet. Leave to rest for 10 minutes. Switch the oven onto 180℃ and bake for 10-15 minutes. Once browned, remove the sticks and start snacking!

MAKES 25 SERVINGS

 THE TERM "UMAMI" DESCRIBES THE FLAVOUR COMMON TO SAVOURY PRODUCTS SUCH AS MUSHROOMS, MEAT AND CHEESE. UMAMI IS ONE OF THE FIVE GENERALLY RECOGNISED BASIC TASTES, WHICH INCLUDES SWEET, SOUR, BITTER AND SALTY.

WHITE PEPPER CARPACCIO

& homemade mayo

Yes, Carpaccio was invented by *Harry's Bar* in Venice but I would say perfected by Roché. A generous crust of white pepper instead of black pepper is a nice change, and allow the fillet to sit in the freezer for a while longer so that when you slice it (preferably on a meat slicer) it holds its shape and looks super-professional!

300g fillet • white pepper & salt for seasoning • olive oil for basting

Tie the fillet with some string to keep its shape. Heat the griddle pan until smoking. Sprinkle salt and white pepper onto a large chopping board. Roll the fillet over the chopping board to cover it with salt and pepper. Brush the fillet on all sides with olive oil and sear it in the griddle pan for no more than 2 minutes, you just want to char, not cook all the way through. Using clingwrap, wrap the fillet tightly into a roll and freeze for at least 45 minutes.

for the mayonnaise:
2 large egg yolks • 2T Dijon mustard • 2t lemon juice • 1t red wine vinegar • ½t Tabasco sauce • ½t salt • ½ cup olive oil • ½ cup vegetable oil

Put all the ingredients (except the oils) in a food processor and blend for 30 seconds. With the blade still spinning, drizzle the oils in very slowly and in a steady stream - this should take about 2 minutes. Process until the mayo is thick and creamy, then refrigerate.

to serve:
2T mayonnaise • a handful of rocket • salt & pepper to taste • 2T capers • balsamic vinegar to drizzle

Cut the fillet into wafer thin slices. Lay the pieces out on a serving plate over a bed of rocket. Sprinkle with salt and pepper. Sprinkle over the capers and drizzle with your homemade mayo and some balsamic vinegar.

SERVES 10

BBQ DEBONED QUAIL

with fennel skewered potatoes

If you find Roché in the kitchen at parties, then you'll find Greg with a pair of tongs in his hand manning the BBQ. One weekend I phoned Greg to see how they were doing. They were at our shared beach cottage and Greg spent 10 minutes telling me about this recipe… how he had marinated it, cooked it and eaten it with gusto. Never be afraid of quail, it's a delicious bird and Greg knows how to cook one!

for the quail marinade:
1½ cups extra virgin olive oil
• ½ cup balsamic vinegar • 1T dried thyme • 2T freshly ground black pepper • 2T honey • 6 semi-boneless quails

Mix all the marinade ingredients together and marinade the quails overnight.

for the skewered potatoes:
1T salt • 1kg small potatoes • ¾ cup extra virgin olive oil • 2T ground fennel seeds • 2 spring onions, chopped • 1T Dijon mustard

Bring a large pot of water to the boil. Add 1T salt and the potatoes and bring back to the boil. Cook for 6 minutes. Drain the potatoes and allow to cool slightly. Cut the potatoes into rounds, about 1½cm thick. Slide the potato rounds onto skewers (if using timber skewers, soak them in water for an hour). Combine the olive oil, fennel, spring onions and mustard and coat the potatoes, leaving them to marinade for an hour or two.

Light up the barbie or heat a griddle pan. Once the fire is ready, place the potatoes on the grill and cook. Turn occasionally until the potatoes are tender and browned – roughly 15 minutes. Don't forget to baste with the marinade! Halfway through grilling the potatoes, add the quails to the grill. Place them breast side down and cook unmoved for 5 minutes until golden brown. Then turn the quails and cook for a further 3 minutes until cooked to medium, basting occasionally.

SERVES 6

ZUCCHINI ROLLS

stuffed with ricotta

Roché and my mate, Simon, flew off to Plett some time back and did a 3-day cheesemaking course, so it's no surprise that she made her own Ricotta for this vegetarian option.

for the tomato sauce:
1T olive oil • 2 anchovy fillets, mashed • 1 garlic clove, chopped • 1 tin (420g) tomatoes, whole & peeled • 1T parsley, chopped • 2T basil, chopped roughly • 1T sugar • 50ml water • salt & black pepper to taste

Heat the oil and melt the anchovies. Add garlic and fry for a few seconds. Add tomatoes, parsley, basil, sugar, water, salt and pepper. Cook down slowly for 30 minutes until you have a thick paste.

for the filling:
1½ cups ricotta • 1/8t nutmeg • 1 egg yolk • salt & black pepper to taste

Beat the ricotta, nutmeg, egg yolk, salt and black pepper together until smooth.

to prepare:
6 zucchinis, sliced thinly lengthways • olive oil for basting • tomato sauce filling • 100g Parmesan, grated

Preheat the oven to 200˚C. Brush the zucchinis with olive oil. Heat a griddle pan and char the zucchinis on each side for about 4 minutes. Pour the tomato sauce into the base of a baking dish. Place a teaspoon of filling onto each zucchini; roll up and secure with a toothpick. Lay the zucchini with the cut side facing upwards, onto the tomato base. Grate over some Parmesan and cover lightly with tinfoil. Bake in the oven for 15 minutes just before serving.

SERVES 4-6

THE TERMS "BIG WHEEL" AND "BIG CHEESE" ORIGINALLY REFERRED TO THOSE WHO WERE WEALTHY ENOUGH TO PURCHASE A WHOLE WHEEL OF CHEESE.

L-R: 1. CERAMIC "SHY GIRL" BY FRANCOIS VAN REENAN 2. GERMAN 1950'S CERAMIC VASE & AN OLD APOTHECARY JAR 3. GREG & ROCHÉ'S BACK GARDEN DESIGNED BY CLINTON POTGIETER
4. JASMINE LINING THE WALLS OUTSIDE 5. SCULPTURE BY RHETT MARTIN 6. COPPER FILIGREE CUPBOARD BY EGG DESIGN *OPPOSITE:* COPY OF THE ORIGINAL "FUR CLOAK" PAINTING BY RUBENS

SQUID INK & PRAWN RAVIOLI

for the stock:
500g sole fish bones • 1 onion, chopped roughly • 1 celery stalk, chopped roughly • 12 tomatoes, squashed • 2 bay leaves • a few parsley stalks • 10 black pepper corns • 1 fennel bulb, chopped • 100ml dry white wine

Put everything into a pot and cover with cold water. Bring to just under a boil, then turn down to simmer. Skim scum off the top frequently. Simmer for 1 hour, then turn off the heat and allow to settle. Pour into a sieve lined with muslin. Freeze your stock and when you need it, defrost it through a muslin-lined sieve at room temperature. By doing this you will end up with a perfectly clear stock.

for the squid ink pasta:
2 cups (500g) flour • a pinch of salt • 3 large eggs plus 2 egg yolks • 16g squid ink

Sieve flour into a clean bowl and turn it onto a counter. Make a well in the centre, season with salt and crack the eggs into it. Add the squid ink and break the egg yolks by stirring with your fingers in a circular motion, slowly incorporating the flour. Bring it together into a ball. Push and fold (knead) for 10 minutes, until the dough is springy but firm. Divide the dough into balls, wrap each in cling wrap and allow to rest in the fridge for 1 hour.

prawn filling:
400g prawns, cold, dried and peeled • 1T parsley, chopped • 45g spinach, chopped • ½t paprika • 2T double cream • 1 garlic clove, chopped

Add all the ingredients (except the cream) into a blender. Pulse (stop and start motion) to chop, then switch off blender. Once roughly chopped, slowly add cream with the motor running for 3 seconds.

SERVES 4-6

 IF YOU ARRIVED AT GREG & ROCHÉ'S FOR A QUICK DRINK AFTER WORK, WITHIN NO TIME THEY'D HAVE RUSTLED UP SOME PASTA DISH USING THEIR HOME-CURED PANCETTA... QUICK, CASUAL AND DELICIOUS. HOWEVER, IF YOU ARE INVITED TO A SATURDAY LUNCH, EXPECT A REAL LABOUR OF LOVE, LIKE THESE RAVIOLIS. THE PRAWN FILLING IS A REVELATION... (THE WEIRD THING IS THAT ROCHÉ DOESN'T EAT SEAFOOD, BUT DELIGHTS IN MAKING THIS FOR HER FRIENDS WHO DO. SWEET HEY!)

for the pasta: dough balls from the fridge • flour for dusting • prawn filling • egg wash • salt for seasoning

Divide each ball into 2 and roll each piece through your pasta machine on the thinnest setting. Dust a 12-piece ravioli tray with flour. Lay a sheet of dough over the tray. Place 1t of filling in each compartment. Brush with egg wash (beaten egg) and lay another sheet over it. Push down into the edges (see picture) and then roll over with a small rolling pin. Tip the ravioli tray over to release. Use a ravioli cutting-wheel to separate the individual pieces. Bring a large pot of water to the boil. Salt it and cook the ravioli for 4 minutes. To serve, put the ravioli in a bowl and ladle over the warmed stock.

SWEET POTATO GNOCCHI

with a warm salsa verde

This warm salsa verde, lightly coated over freshly made tagliatelle, is something Roché made at our beach cottage and has since proven to be an equally successful partner with sweet potato gnocchi.

for the gnocchi:
1kg orange sweet potatoes
• salt & black pepper for seasoning
• 2 small eggs • 350g flour
• extra flour for rolling

Boil the potatoes in their jackets until tender. Drain and return to the pan for 1 minute to dry them out. Peel the skins while still hot and put them through a potato ricer (or mash manually). A ricer will give you a much lighter texture and is a worthwhile kitchen investment. Season and mix in with the eggs. Now sprinkle over half the flour. Knead by folding the edges over and over into the centre. Add the remaining flour and fold in. Don't overwork the dough. Roll out the dough into one sausage shape and then cut it into 3cm lengths. Now roll these lengths out into sausage shapes again and chop the dough into 2cm lengths. Press each piece of dough against the back of a fork, so that it curves slightly and leaves indentations, which will help the gnocchi hold the accompanying sauce. In a large pasta pot, bring salted water to a rolling boil. Drop 8-10 gnocchi into the water. Gnocchi is considered ready when it rises to the surface.

for the salsa verde:
5T Italian parsley • 130g capers
• 4 large anchovies • 2 red chillies
**• juice of 1 lemon • ¾ cup (185ml)
olive oil**

Chop up all the ingredients finely. Pour the olive oil into a pan, add all the ingredients and allow to warm gently. Add the gnocchi to a dish and spoon over the warm salsa verde before serving.

SERVES 4-6

CRANBERRY JELLY & LIQUORICE ICE-CREAM

This is the dessert of the book. Firstly, it just looks so bloody beautiful. Some turned their noses up at the thought of liquorice ice-cream, but it's Roché's inquisitive, gastronomic intuition that made her experiment with this one… and it's a WINNER! A bag of frozen cranberries is also a worthwhile treat on their own, especially on a hot summer day, with possibly a shot of Grappa!

100g liquorice toffees • 1 cup (250ml) milk • 4 egg yolks • 1 cup (250ml) cream • 1 vanilla pod, deseeded • ½ cup sugar

Put your toffees and milk in a pot and heat to melt the toffee, but do not boil. In a separate bowl beat the egg yolks with sugar until thick. Combine the hot toffee mixture with the egg and sugar mixture, stirring continuously. Put back in the pot and heat gently until it's thickened slightly, but do not boil. Cool and stir in the cream. Transfer to your ice-cream maker and freeze according to the manufacturer's instructions.

MAKES 1½L

for the cranberry jelly: 300g cranberries • 2 cups (500ml) dry white wine • 2 cups (500ml) apple juice • 5 leaves of gelatin • 250g caster sugar

Liquidise cranberries and pass them through a fine sieve to remove any seeds. Heat the wine and apple juice to just below boiling. Soak gelatin leaves in cold water for 5 minutes and wring out. Add caster sugar to the heated wine and juice, and dissolve. Add 1/3 of the wine to the gelatin leaves and stir to dissolve, then add the mixture back into the wine. Add liquidised cranberries and stir well. Pour the mixture equally into moulds and refrigerate to set. Remove from the fridge 15 minutes before serving. This will make it easier to remove from the mould.

SERVES 6

• GETTING TO KNOW ROCHÉ

MY NICKNAME IS Shakey & Ro. **MY EMOTIONAL AGE IS** 32. **I CAN'T STAND** seafood and winter. **WHAT MAKES ME SMILE AND LAUGH ARE** Greg and my children. They are very funny, quirky and left of centre. **MY FAVOURITE PLACE IN SA IS** our beach cottage down the South Coast. **MY FAVOURITE SINGLE THING IN MY HOME IS** a huge William Kentridge charcoal drawing that always makes we wonder who the wonderful waltzing couple are. **THE MEAL I'D PROBABLY SERVE GUESTS IN OUR COUNTRY WOULD BE** a large platter of locally cured meats and cheeses. **MY GUILTIEST PLEASURE IS** reading in the bath for hours. **THE ONE THING ABOUT MY HOME THAT REFLECTS MY INDIVIDUALISM MOST IS** a large collection of curiosities that we cannot stop adding to. **IF MY HOME WERE BURNING DOWN, I'D RUN BACK INSIDE FOR** nothing really. I'm not too concerned about material things, maybe a few pairs of shoes! **THE ONE WORD I'D USE TO SUM UP MY LIFE IS** "splendid".

• GETTING TO KNOW GREG

MY EMOTIONAL AGE IS according to my life partner, 50. **I CAN'T STAND** lies, thieves and most of all, designers that plagiarise and get recognition for it. **WHAT MAKES ME SMILE AND LAUGH IS** mostly myself! I think life is a hoot and find humor in a lot of things, but most recently my kids have developed the most wicked sense of humour. **IN 10 YEARS TIME I WANT TO BE** a better, calmer, softer and less rushed person. And from a design side, hopefully, more prolific and much more mature and experimental. **MY FAVOURITE SINGLE THING IN MY HOME IS** our original Arne Jacobson egg chair. But you can never sit in it 'cos our bullterrier is always sitting there. Boy, he's got good taste! **IF MY HOME WERE BURNING DOWN, I'D RUN BACK INSIDE FOR** a lot! Although we're not material people, I hope to morph into a gigantic squid like creature so my eight arms could grab all the artworks. **THE ONE WORD I'D USE TO SUM UP MY LIFE IS** what Roché claims she's putting on my tombstone... "should of".

i will not eat oysters.
i want my food dead.
not sick.
not wounded.
dead.
- WOODY ALLEN

part of the success in life is to eat what you like and let the food fight it out inside.

MARK TWAIN

ALOHA
KWAZULU-NATAL

TREASURE
ISLAND

pink grapefruit salad with mandarin & fresh coconut
poached chicken salad with rocket & pomegranate seeds
avo, prawn & feta with smoked paprika mayo
ceviche with tortilla chips
tortilla de potata
Brazilian giant kebabs
clams, chorizo & chickpeas
tequila lime chicken wings
rib eye steaks with chimichurri
margarita pipette shooters

Clinton
AKA
'COBRA'

ALOHA

CLINTON POTGIETER (AKA COBRA) IS A MAN OF THE SEA. AN OUTDOOR ENTHUSIAST, NATURE LOVER (ESPECIALLY PLANTS), AND THE MAN CAN WIELD A MEAN PAIR OF BRAAI TONGS. HE IS ALMOST A PART OF MY FAMILY…

In fact he made my son Tyler's school news pages… "My dad's friend Clint (we call him Cobra) took us to a beach cottage and we played softball and went for walks on the beach and Cobra went surfing." Cobra is actually a very big kid. At the drop of a hat, he'll pack his bakkie with surfboards (including a long board), skim boards, a baseball set, soccer balls, a wetsuit and his spear gun… oh, and maybe the kayak thrown onto the roof.

He's the ultimate man's man (with a huge soft spot for women who speak foreign languages). I met Cobra when he landscaped the citrus orchard on our property and, since then, we have shared many wild and wonderful evenings out and weekends away. With business interests in Mozambique, it's only natural that a cooler box would return with mud crabs, glorious clams and prawns so fresh they still have their feelers on… and then we cook. My only criticism is that Cobra has promised freshly picked mussels (arrived back with 12 … what can I do with 12!), and when he did spearfish, he arrived back with the tiniest fish ever… and as yet… no crayfish!

His love of travel has taken him from places as diverse as Petra in Jordan to trance parties in the Transkei… but his love for Latin America and beach life is obvious… and that's what you will find in these inspired recipes… a whole lot of va-va-voom with a dash of COBRA!

1. CLINTON'S UBER COOL FLORIDA ROAD COURTYARD 2. COBRA'S GOT GAME… EVEN WEARING HIS KITSCH KENYAN FISHING SHIRT 3. SHELLS FROM MADAGASCAR 4. THE REGISTRATION PLATE OF HIS "FUTURE CAR" 5. COBRA'S "FAMILY" 6. A COLLECTION OF SURF MAGS, TRAVEL & WINE BOOKS 7. MAIDEN FROM MOZAMBIQUE 8. THE REMNANTS OF COBRA'S INFAMOUS COCKTAILS 9. A 100 YEAR OLD CAGE FROM AN OLD SHIP 10. COBRA'S PRIZED POSSESSION, HIS FIG TREE 11. ONE OF HIS MANY ORCHIDS 12. COBRA'S "DEPARTMENT STORE" CLOTHING RACK 13. THE GREEN FINGER STRIKES AGAIN! 14. STILL A KID AT HEART, CLINTON SHOWS OFF HIS VINTAGE COLLECTION OF OLD CHILDREN'S BOOKS 15. COBRA'S PLACEMAT 16. THE ELIGIBLE BACHELOR HIMSELF. *For captions relevant to other pictures in this chapter, please refer to the Addendum.*

PINK GRAPEFRUIT SALAD

with mandarin & fresh coconut

We South Africans are blessed with an abundance of fruit, especially citrus. Cobra's medley of grapefruit, mandarin, orange and fresh coconut really "comes alive" with this zingy lime and chilli dressing.

for the salad:
350g of citrus (pink grapefruit, mandarins and oranges)
• fresh coconut, chopped

for the dressing:
1t fish sauce • 2t white sugar
• 2 red chillies, chopped finely
• 4 limes, juiced

Make the dressing by adding the fish sauce, sugar and chillies to the lime juice and mix well. Arrange the fruit on a platter and pour over the dressing. (You can add some olives if you wish.)

SERVES 2

 BETWEEN 1795 AND 1815, BRITISH SAILORS WERE REQUIRED TO CONSUME A DAILY RATION OF LIME JUICE, ALONG WITH THEIR DAILY RATION OF RUM, WHICH IS WHY BRITISH SEAMEN BECAME KNOWN AS LIMEYS.

POACHED CHICKEN SALAD

with rocket & pomegranate seeds

Fresh pomegranate seeds display their jewel-like appearance during the SA winter. Snap them up when you see them.

4 chicken thighs • 4 handfuls of rocket • a small handful of roasted peanuts • a big handful of pomegranate seeds • 12 spring onions

Poach the chicken by adding the thighs to cold water. Bring the water to the boil and then turn off the heat, leaving the chicken in the water for 45 minutes. Remove, pat dry and shred the chicken with a fork. Now lay down some rocket onto a plate, distribute the chicken, roasted peanuts, pomegranate seeds and spring onions. Drizzle with a chilli and lime dressing (see opposite page for dressing recipe).

accompaniments:
avo, prawn, feta & roasted pumpkin seeds with smoked paprika mayo

Like love and marriage, these ingredients just click. And they make a great DIY salad. Not a recipe at all, but an idea... scoop the avocado flesh out with a teaspoon into "ball" shapes. Squeeze over a little lime juice, sprinkle with green pumpkin seeds and feta before adding the cooked and peeled prawns.

for the mayo:
1t smoked paprika • 4T good quality mayonnaise • 1T olive oil • juice of 1 lime

Mix like crazy until well blended. That's it, folks.

SERVES 4

THE AVOCADO GETS ITS NAME FROM THE LATIN AMERICAN "NAHUATL AHUACATL" MEANING "TESTICLE", REFERRING TO ITS SHAPE.

L-R: 1. NO NEED FOR A BUNCH OF COSMETICS TO LOOK GOOD...HE'S 'AU NATURAL' 2. THE BREAKFAST FOR CHAMPIONS! 3. UPSTAIRS PATIO WHERE THINGS OFTEN GET MESSY 4. OUTSIDE SHOWER & BEACH GEAR WASH UP 5. WHERE "THE MAGIC" HAPPENS 6. COBRA'S GOT BALLS... AND HE LOVES PLAYING TENNIS WITH THEM *OPPOSITE:* MORE OF COBRA'S OLD CHILDREN'S BOOKS

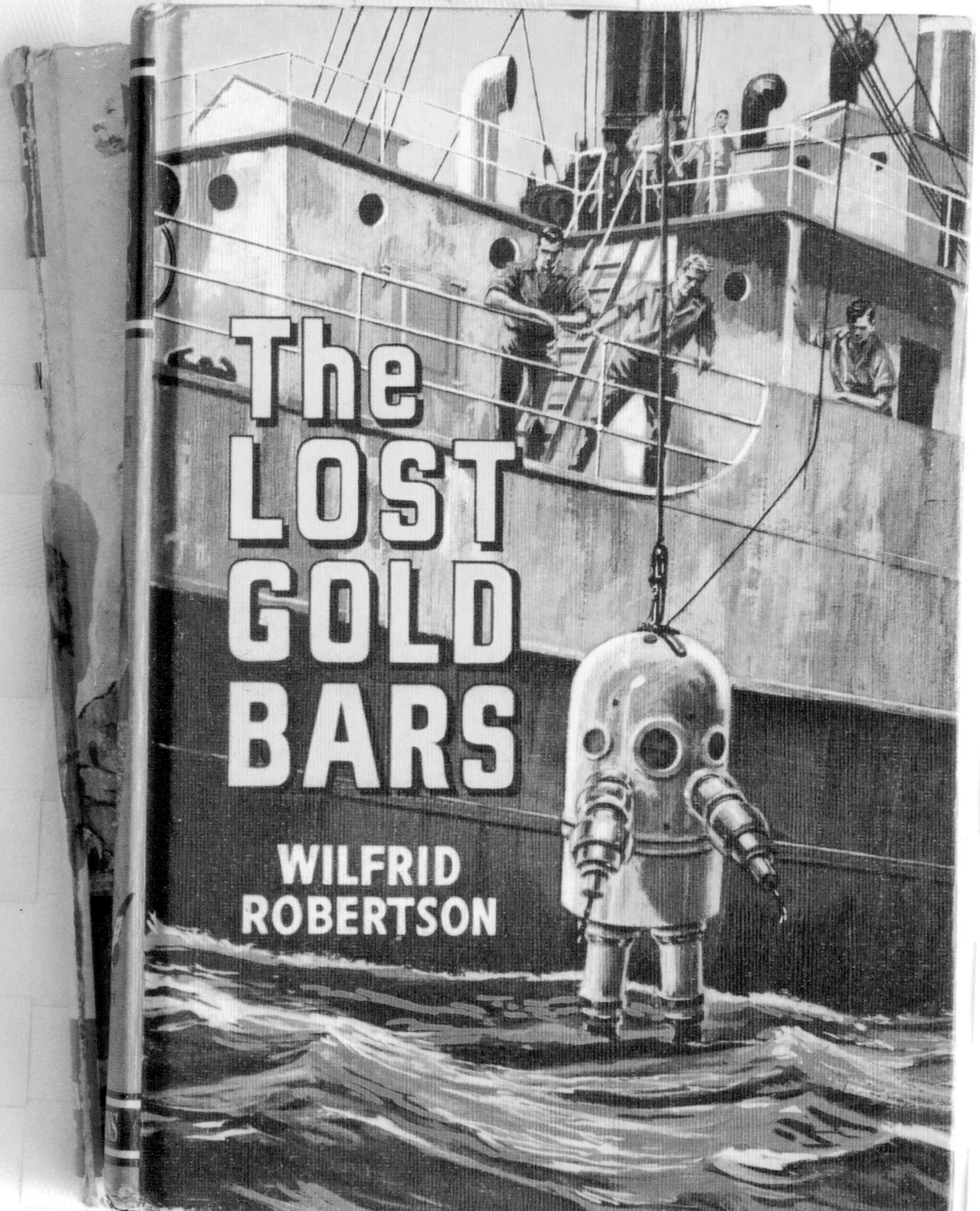
The LOST GOLD BARS
WILFRID ROBERTSON

CEVICHE WITH TORTILLA CHIPS

Do not even attempt to make this with frozen hake. You will not get any Central American street-cred if you do. We found fresh Dorado (as Cobra says, "it's the chicken of the sea, because it tastes so good"). The best ceviche I've ever eaten was on the beach at Caye Caulker, an island off Belize. The seafood they used was Conch. Strange, but true…

350g dorado or cape salmon
• juice of 6 lemons • 1T coriander,
chopped • 2t garlic, chopped finely
• 2 red chillies, chopped finely
• 1t dried oregano

Slice the fish into bite-size pieces, about 5mm thick and transfer to a non-metallic dish. Add the balance of the ingredients and stir.

Place in the fridge for at least 30 minutes. Strain the fish through a colander, reserving the "tiger milk", which you can serve in a separate dish. Serve with corn tortilla chips (and tequila!).

SERVES 4

THE TORTILLA CHIP WAS POPULARISED BY REBECCA WEBB CARRANZA AS A WAY TO MAKE USE OF MISSHAPEN TORTILLAS REJECTED FROM HER FACTORY'S AUTOMATED TORTILLA MANUFACTURING MACHINE.

TORTILLA DE POTATA

Tortillas are perfect for a one-pan breakfast dish…

1 large onion, chopped • 1t garlic, chopped finely • 1t ginger, grated finely • 1/8 cup (30ml) olive oil • 4 large potatoes, boiled and sliced into 5mm slices • 4 ears of sweetcorn, trimmed of their corn • 6 eggs • 2t salt

for serving:
3T thick Greek yoghurt
• 2 spring onions, chopped

Fry the onion, garlic and ginger in the oil until translucent. Add the slices of cooked potatoes and the corn and stir-fry gently for 5 minutes. Beat the eggs with the salt and pour over the potato mixture. Place in a preheated oven at 180°C for 50 minutes. Cut into wedges and serve with the Greek yoghurt mixed with chopped spring onions.

SERVES 6

CLINT SAYS

DID YOU KNOW? BRAZIL BORDERS EVERY COUNTRY
IN SOUTH AMERICA EXCEPT CHILE AND ECUADOR.

SHP244

BRAZILIAN GIANT KEBABS

If you ask Cobra for one memorable meal experienced in Central/South America, he will automatically mention the giant meat kebabs in Brazil. He is such a boykie… in fact, so convinced was Cobra to replicate this on SA soil, that he traced down these giant metal kebab skewers from a hardware store in Maputo. I have added in my kofta recipe here, more Middle Eastern than Brazilian but "Brazziliant" all the same.

lamb, apricot & bay leaves:
500g (4) lamb loin cuts • 120g dried apricots • 8 bay leaves

Soak the bay leaves and the apricots in water first to help prevent burning. Then thread onto the skewer (check the pic for design tips, but be creative in your own way!) and BBQ away.

kofta & aubergine:
550g lamb, minced • 1T parsley, chopped • 1T coriander, chopped • 1t paprika • 1t cumin, ground • 3 garlic cloves, chopped finely • 1 green chilli, chopped finely • 1t salt • 1t cracked black pepper • 4 small aubergines

Make the kofta by mixing all the ingredients (except the aubergines) thoroughly by hand, squeezing the meat between your fingers. You almost need to knead the mince, as you would bread dough, to amalgamate the proteins so they stick onto the skewer blades. Thread the halved aubergines onto skewers, alternating the lamb mince between the aubergines. BBQ over medium coals, turning frequently but gently so that the lamb does not separate from the skewers.

rump & dried apple:
500g (3) rump steaks • 120g dried apple slices (soaked in water first) • olive oil for drizzling • oregano for seasoning

Thread the rump between the apple slices. Brush with olive oil and sprinkle with oregano. Be creative and mix and match different vegetables to create your very own veggie kebab!

EACH RECIPE SERVES 4 & MAKES 2 LARGE KEBABS

CLAMS, CHORIZO & CHICKPEAS

Clint does business in Maputo and, before heading back to Durban, he fills up a cooler box with clams & fresh prawns from the Maputo fish market. Chorizo and clams are a perfect match, but the secret ingredient here is the smoked paprika… you will need some fresh Portuguese rolls to suck up the tasty juices.

1/3 cup (80ml) olive oil • 1 onion, chopped finely • 3 garlic cloves, chopped roughly • 1t ginger, grated • 3 red chillies, chopped finely • 1t smoked paprika • 3 bay leaves • 125g chorizo sausage, sliced • 36 clams • 1 cup (250ml) quality white wine • 425g tinned tomatoes, chopped • 400g tinned chickpeas, rinsed and drained • 1T flat leaf parsley, chopped finely

Fry the onion in the olive oil until translucent. Now add all the aromatics and the chorizo. Stir-fry for a good 5 minutes to release the oils and flavour from the chorizo. Now add the clams, the white wine, tomatoes, chickpeas and parsley. Put the lid on the pot and shake to mix all the ingredients together. Steam for an additional 10 minutes until all the clams have opened up. (Discard any unopened clams.) Serve with bread and eat the clams with your fingers. "It's messy, so don't cook this on a first date" is Cobra's advice.

SERVES 6

CLAMS, LIKE OYSTERS, HAVE NO EYES, EARS OR NOSES, SO THEY CANNOT SEE, HEAR, OR SMELL.

TEQUILA LIME CHICKEN WINGS

In essence, these are Margarita wings, ideally marinated overnight. You char-grill the wings and then reduce the sauce down to a sticky marmalade. One tequila wing, two tequila wings, three tequila wings, FLOOR!

½ cup (125ml) tequila • ½ cup (125ml) freshly squeezed orange juice • ½ cup (125ml) lime juice, freshly squeezed • 1t cumin, ground • zest of 2 oranges • 2 garlic cloves, crushed finely • 80ml runny honey • 12 chicken wings

Mix all the marinade ingredients together, ensuring you dissolve the honey. Add the wings, cover with clingfilm and marinade overnight (about 8 hours). Drain the wings and pat dry. Char-grill over medium coals for 12–15 minutes, turning frequently and ensuring they do not burn. (Be vigilant... they catch easily!) Add the marinade to a frying pan and reduce until sugary and sticky. Add the wings to the pan off the BBQ, and coat them in the sticky mess. Serve with lemon/lime cheeks and cumin flavoured salt. Yum! You could serve sticks of celery and a blue cheese dressing if you wanted to Americanize it!

SERVES 4

 IT'S A COMMON MISCONCEPTION THAT SOME TEQUILAS CONTAIN AN ACTUAL WORM IN THE BOTTLE. ONLY CERTAIN MEZCALS (AN INFERIOR VERSION OF TEQUILA) WERE EVER SOLD "CON GUSANO", MEANING "WITH WORM", WHICH STARTED AS A MARKETING GIMMICK IN THE 1940S.

RIB EYE STEAKS WITH CHIMICHURRI

Chimichurri is one of Argentina's national sauces, perfect on steak or fish or even char-grilled vegetables. In essence, it's a raw onion and red wine vinegar salsa. I have chosen rib eye (also known as Scotch fillet or, in France, as the famous entrecôte) but any steak cut will do.

540g rib eye steak (2 pieces)
• ½ cup (125ml) olive oil • ½ cup (125ml) red wine vinegar • ¼ cup (60ml) water • 1 medium onion, chopped finely • 4 garlic cloves, chopped finely • ½ red pepper, chopped finely • 1 tomato, peeled, deseeded and chopped finely • 1T dried oregano • 1T paprika • 3 bay leaves, sliced finely ("chiffonade", if you want to be posh) • 2 red chillies, chopped finely with seeds • 1t sea salt • 1t freshly ground black pepper

Mix all the marinade ingredients together and let the sauce rest in the fridge overnight to blend all the flavours. (It's even better made 2 to 3 days in advance.) Char-grill your steaks and spoon over at least 2T of the sauce. Flippin' amazing!

SERVES 6

BE WARNED: THIS SAUCE OF COBRA'S IS NOW FIRMLY IN MY REPERTOIRE OF WOW! SAUCES. EVERYONE ON THIS SHOOT WENT MAD FOR IT... AS WILL YOU. I THINK BRAAIS HAVE CHANGED FOREVER AS A RESULT.

MARGARITA PIPETTE SHOOTERS

Cobra loves a little drama in his life, so he likes filling these medical lab purchased pipettes with margarita mix and jamming them into crushed ice. Great to kick-start a party, or to cleanse the palate between courses. Each pipette takes 80ml and the proportions are:

2 shots (90ml) tequila • 1 shot (45ml) triple sec • 1 shot (45ml) freshly squeezed lime juice (so if you're catering for 6 people you will need 540ml tequila • 270ml triple sec • 270ml fresh lime juice)

Shake in a cocktail shaker with ice and strain into the pipettes. Rim the edges of the pipettes with salt and serve to your thirsty guests.

"IF LIFE GIVES YOU LIMES… MAKE MARGARITAS!"
- JIMMY BUFFETT

WHAT IS CLINTON'S...

NICKNAME? FAT COBRA. AGE? I thought I was 33 for most of this year but only recently discovered I was actually 32... stoked! SIGN? JOB? Gardener. LOVE? Moustaches. FAVOURITE SMELL? Beach. ONE THING THAT MAKES HIM SMILE & LAUGH? What always cracks me up are the changing hairstyles of my dad's little schnauzers. FAVOURITE PLACE IN SA? Amanzimtoti Southbroom, Southcoast. FAVOURITE PLACE IN THE WORLD? Montecristi, Ecuador. FAVOURITE SINGLE THING IN HIS HOME? My fig tree. DREAM HOME? A shack on the beach, but my current home is a close second. HOBBY? Ping pong. PASSION? My collection of cheap porcelain dogs that I give away as gifts – ask my sis, she loves them (not)! ROOM IN THE HOUSE HE SPENDS MOST OF HIS TIME IN? The toilet. FIRST MEAL HE'D SERVE A GUEST IN OUR COUNTRY? A slab of our finest cow with chimichurri. STUFF HE'D RUN BACK INSIDE FOR IF HIS HOUSE WAS BURNING DOWN? My girlfriend (if I had one) and my photo journals. ONE WORD HE'D USE TO SUM UP HIS LIFE? Bizarre.

my favourite animal is steak.

– FRAN LEBOWITZ

**great food
is like
great sex.
the more
you have
the more
you want.**
GAEL GREENE

OHA - ZN

KWAZULU-NATAL

SANS1116 SABS 503

SHP257

AN OLIVE TREE CAN LIVE UP TO 1500 YEARS.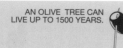

A BEAN HAS MORE DNA PER CELL THAN A HUMAN CELL.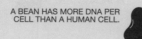

CHINA PRODUCES MORE APPLES THAN THE REST OF THE WORLD.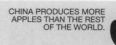

BEES CANNOT RECOGNISE THE COLOUR RED.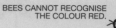

 THERE ARE ABOUT 50 SPECIES OF FISH THAT CAN FLY OR GLIDE.

GRAPES AND EGGS WILL EXPLODE IN THE MICROWAVE.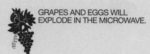

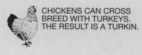 CHICKENS CAN CROSS BREED WITH TURKEYS. THE RESULT IS A TURKIN.

 THE FEAR OF PEANUT BUTTER STICKING TO THE ROOF OF THE MOUTH IS CALLED ARACHIBUTYROPHOBIA.

TURNIP SEEDS CAN INCREASE THEIR WEIGHT 15 TIMES A MINUTE AND IN RICH SOIL THEY MAY INCREASE THEIR WEIGHT 15000 TIMES A DAY.

SCANDINAVIAN TRADITIONS HOLD THAT IF A BOY AND GIRL EAT FROM THE SAME LOAF, THEY ARE BOUND TO FALL IN LOVE.

STALKS OF SUGAR CANE CAN REACH UP TO 30FT.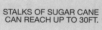

THE BLUE RINGS OF THE BLUE-RINGED OCTOPUS ARE VISIBLE ONLY WHEN IT IS ABOUT TO ATTACK.

 AN EGG CONTAINS ALL VITAMINS EXCEPT FOR THE VITAMIN C.

 AN OYSTER CAN CHANGE ITS GENDER.

THE WRECK OF THE TITANIC HOLDS THE OLDEST WINE CELLAR IN THE WORLD.

THERE ARE NO BLOSSOMS ON THE BRANCHES OF A FIG TREE, INSTEAD IT'S INSIDE THE FRUIT.

DURING YOUR LIFETIME YOU WILL EAT ABOUT THE WEIGHT OF 6 FULL GROWN ELEPHANTS.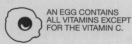

THE PRIMARY REASON FOR GROWING LINSEED WAS TO PRODUCE ITS FIBRE FOR MAKING LINEN AND ROPE.

THERE ARE ABOUT 15000 VARIETIES OF RICE.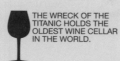

IF YOU EAT ONIONS YOU CAN GET RID OF ONION BREATH BY EATING PARSLEY.

 ALBATROSSES CAN SLEEP WHILE THEY ARE FLYING.

EARLY EYGPTIAN WRITINGS URGED MOTHERS TO SEND THEIR CHILDREN TO SCHOOL WITH PLENTY OF BREAD AND BEER FOR LUNCH.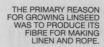

ALMONDS ARE ACTUALLY STONE FRUITS RELATED TO CHERRIES, PEACHES AND PLUMS.

AIR IS AN IMPORTANT INGREDIENT IN ICE-CREAM - IT KEEPS THE ICE-CREAM FROM FREEZING SOLID.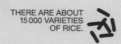

ONE WAY TO TELL THE AGE OF A FISH IS BY LOOKING AT ITS SCALES. THEY HAVE GROWTH RINGS JUST LIKE TREES.

NUTMEG IS NOT A FRUIT, BUT THE KERNEL OF AN APRICOT-LIKE FRUIT.

DUCKS HAVE THREE EYELIDS.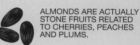

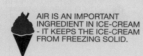 AN APPLE IS COVERED IN A THIN LAYER OF WAX.

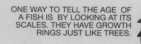 A PREGNANT GOLDFISH IS CALLED A TWIT.

ROCKET HAS BEEN GROWN IN THE MEDITERRANEAN AREA SINCE ROMAN TIMES, AND IS CONSIDERED AN APHRODISIAC.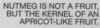

ESKIMOS USE REFRIGERATORS TO KEEP THEIR FOOD FROM FREEZING.

RESEARCH ON PIGS LED TO THE DEVELOPMENT OF CAT SCANS.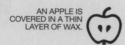

ANCIENT GREEK WOMEN MADE A TYPE OF BLUSH BY PAINTING THEIR CHEEKS WITH PASTES MADE OUT OF CRUSHED BERRIES AND SEEDS.

CAESAR SALAD IS NOT NAMED AFTER JULIUS CAESAR, BUT AFTER CHEF CAESAR CARDINI.

AN OSTRICH'S EYE IS BIGGER THAN ITS BRAIN.

MALE HORSES HAVE MORE TEETH THAN FEMALE HORSES. MALES HAVE 40 WHILE FEMALES HAVE 36.

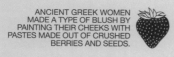 MORE THAN 25% OF THE WORLD'S RAINFORESTS ARE IN BRAZIL.

YOU USE MORE CALORIES EATING CELERY THAN THERE ARE IN THE CELERY ITSELF.

A GIANT SQUID HAS THE LARGEST EYES IN THE WORLD.

GARLIC IS ACTUALLY CONSIDERED BOTH A VEGETABLE AND A HERB.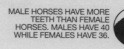

THERE ARE MORE CHICKENS ON EARTH THAN THERE ARE HUMANS.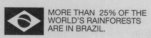

BANANAS ARE ONE OF THE BEST SOURCES OF POTASSIUM.

WATERMELON CONSISTS OF 92% WATER & 8% SUGAR.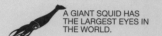

RAW HONEY DOES NOT SPOIL.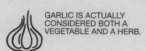

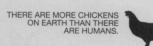 THERE ARE ABOUT 1 BILLION SHEEP ON THE PLANET.

BLACK PEPPER IS THE MOST POPULAR SPICE IN THE WORLD.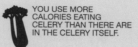

HORSES ARE ABLE TO CLIMB STRAIGHT STAIRCASES, BUT NOT CIRCULAR ONES.

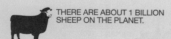

COLOUR IS NOT AN INDICATOR FOR THE TASTE OR RIPENESS IN CRANBERRIES.

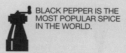

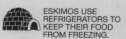

THE COCONUT MOST LIKELY ORIGINATED SOMEWHERE AROUND NEW GUINEA IN THE PACIFIC OCEAN.

ARGENTINA IS THE WORLD'S MAJOR PRODUCER OF WHEAT, BEANS, MAIZE, SOYBEANS, BEEF AND MILK.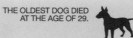

THE OLDEST DOG DIED AT THE AGE OF 29.

CAMEL'S MILK, WHICH IS WIDELY DRUNK IN ARAB COUNTRIES, HAS 10 TIMES MORE IRON THAN COW'S MILK.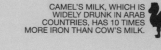

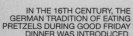 MEL BLANC (VOICE OF BUGS BUNNY) WAS ALLERGIC TO CARROTS.

 MILK IS SOMETIMES CALLED NATURE'S MOST NEARLY PERFECT FOOD.

BLACK OLIVES CONTAIN (ON AVERAGE) 10-30% MORE OIL THAN GREEN OLIVES.

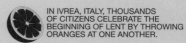 THE BEST-VALUE CONSUMER PURCHASE, IN TERMS OF THE PRICE AND USAGE, IS AN ELECTRIC KETTLE.

IN THE 16TH CENTURY, THE GERMAN TRADITION OF EATING PRETZELS DURING GOOD FRIDAY DINNER WAS INTRODUCED.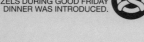

PIGS CAN'T LOOK UP AT THE SKY.

IF YOU CAN SEE A RAINBOW YOU MUST HAVE YOUR BACK TO THE SUN.

TERMITES EAT WOOD TWICE AS FAST WHEN LISTENING TO HEAVY METAL MUSIC.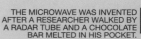

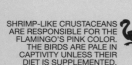 COWS DRINK NEARLY A BATHTUB FULL OF WATER EACH DAY.

A NEW STARFISH MAY BE REGENERATED FROM A SINGLE ARM ATTACHED TO A PORTION OF THE CENTRAL DISK.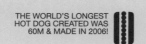

 ONE GLASS OF WATER SHUTS DOWN MIDNIGHT HUNGER PANGS.

IN IVREA, ITALY, THOUSANDS OF CITIZENS CELEBRATE THE BEGINNING OF LENT BY THROWING ORANGES AT ONE ANOTHER.

SHRIMP-LIKE CRUSTACEANS ARE RESPONSIBLE FOR THE FLAMINGO'S PINK COLOR. THE BIRDS ARE PALE IN CAPTIVITY UNLESS THEIR DIET IS SUPPLEMENTED.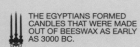

THE WORLD'S LONGEST HOT DOG CREATED WAS 60M & MADE IN 2006!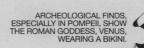

BUTTERFLIES TASTE WITH THEIR FEET.

THE MICROWAVE WAS INVENTED AFTER A RESEARCHER WALKED BY A RADAR TUBE AND A CHOCOLATE BAR MELTED IN HIS POCKET.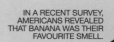

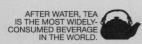 THE EGYPTIANS FORMED CANDLES THAT WERE MADE OUT OF BEESWAX AS EARLY AS 3000 BC.

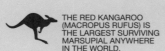 THE RED KANGAROO (MACROPUS RUFUS) IS THE LARGEST SURVIVING MARSUPIAL ANYWHERE IN THE WORLD.

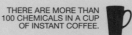 THE CATFISH HAS OVER 27000 TASTE BUDS. (WHAT COULD BE SO TASTY ON THE BOTTOM OF A POND?)

DONALD DUCK COMICS WERE BANNED IN FINLAND BECAUSE HE DIDN'T WEAR PANTS.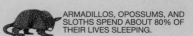

 AFTER WATER, TEA IS THE MOST WIDELY-CONSUMED BEVERAGE IN THE WORLD.

ARCHEOLOGICAL FINDS, ESPECIALLY IN POMPEII, SHOW THE ROMAN GODDESS, VENUS, WEARING A BIKINI.

THERE ARE MORE THAN 100 CHEMICALS IN A CUP OF INSTANT COFFEE.

IN A RECENT SURVEY, AMERICANS REVEALED THAT BANANA WAS THEIR FAVOURITE SMELL.

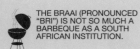 THE BRAAI (PRONOUNCED "BRI") IS NOT SO MUCH A BARBEQUE AS A SOUTH AFRICAN INSTITUTION.

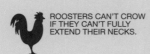 ROOSTERS CAN'T CROW IF THEY CAN'T FULLY EXTEND THEIR NECKS.

IN 1850 THE FIRST WASHING MACHINE WAS INVENTED. IT WAS A WOODEN MACHINE WITH A HAND-TURNED WHEEL THAT SPLASHED WATER ON DISHES.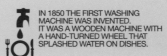

ARMADILLOS, OPOSSUMS, AND SLOTHS SPEND ABOUT 80% OF THEIR LIVES SLEEPING.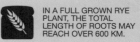

THE FIRST ELECTRIC MIXER WAS INVENTED BY HERBERT JOHNSTON IN 1908 AND SOLD BY THE KITCHEN AID DIVISION OF THE HOBART MANUFACTURING COMPANY.

NO TECHNICAL CREW MEMBER EVER EATS THE SAME AIRLINE MEAL AS A COLLEAGUE, TO MINIMIZE THE RISK OF ALL PILOTS ON BOARD BEING ILL.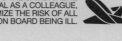

THE STRONGEST MUSCLE IN THE BODY IS THE TONGUE.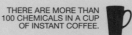

PORCUPINES FLOAT IN WATER.

 THE EARLIEST REFERENCE TO A CORKSCREW IS, "STEEL WORM USED FOR THE DRAWING OF CORKS OUT OF BOTTLES" FROM 1681.

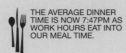 THE AVERAGE DINNER TIME IS NOW 7:47PM AS WORK HOURS EAT INTO OUR MEAL TIME.

 HUMANS AND DOLPHINS ARE THE ONLY SPECIES THAT HAVE SEX FOR PLEASURE.

IN A FULL GROWN RYE PLANT, THE TOTAL LENGTH OF ROOTS MAY REACH OVER 600 KM.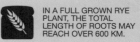

CROCODILES ARE THE MOST INTELLIGENT OF REPTILES, BUT A CROCODILE CANNOT STICK OUT ITS TONGUE.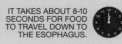

IT TAKES ABOUT 8-10 SECONDS FOR FOOD TO TRAVEL DOWN TO THE ESOPHAGUS.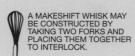

PEARLS MELT IN VINEGAR.

SWEET CORN IS USUALLY SHORTER THAN FIELD-CORN VARIETIES.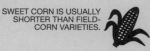

 THE MALE AND NOT THE FEMALE SEAHORSE CARRIES THE EGGS AND GIVES BIRTH.

A MAKESHIFT WHISK MAY BE CONSTRUCTED BY TAKING TWO FORKS AND PLACING THEM TOGETHER TO INTERLOCK.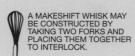

 SNAILS CAN SLEEP FOR 3 YEARS WITHOUT EATING.

THE SEEDS OF AN INDIAN LOTUS TREE REMAIN VIABLE FOR 300 TO 400 YEARS.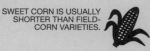

PHOTOGRAPHIC CONTRIBUTOR:
Tony Christie

AIOLI:
As continued from page 19
1 egg yolk • 3 garlic cloves, chopped roughly
• 1t Dijon mustard • 2 garlic cloves, pounded to
a paste • 300ml olive oil • salt & pepper to taste
• juice from 1 lemon

Whisk the lot (except the lemon juice) while adding
the oil little by little... add the lemon juice at the end
to bring out the flavour.

AUTHENTIC MOUSSAKA:
As continued from page 22
to assemble:
Slice the 3 aubergines in half lengthways and cut
around the outside edges, and scoop out the filling.
Chop the aubergines into 1cm cubes and add to the
meat mixture. Place them cut-side up on a baking
tray and drizzle with olive oil. Bake at 180°C for
15 minutes. Remove from the oven and now start
assembling. Add 1T béchamel to the base of each
halved aubergine. Lay two slices of potato and top
up with the meat mixture, distributing the sauces
evenly amongst the béchamel over the meat sauce
and chuck back in the oven again at 180°C for 25-30
minutes until the béchamel has puffed up and is
golden brown.

ADDITIONAL CAPTIONS
pg 10 (L-R) 1. Tiffany's beautifying things 2. Stash
for their nieces & nephews - who says you can't
buy love?! 3. Self-portrait by artist that Simon
claims has a striking resemblance to his wife. He
bought it because he couldn't stand the thought
of any other man hanging it up on their wall!

pg 24 (L-R) 1. Tiff's favourite jacket, made by
Terrence Bray, hanging on the mirror from her
best friend, George 2. More flower power!
3. Part of their cosy fireplace with "Faces" by
Deryck Healey.

PHOTOGRAPHIC CONTRIBUTOR:
Russel Wasserfall

ADDITIONAL CAPTIONS
pg 36 (L-R) 1. Lucie's loft bedroom. 2. Self-
portrait of Lucie lying on the rocks in Bakoven.
3. The artist at work in her studio.

PHOTOGRAPHIC CONTRIBUTORS:
**Russel Wasserfall, Adriaan Louw, Ray du Toit,
Michael Bowles & Mark Williams**

ROAST CHICKEN WITH LEMON, GARLIC &
ROSEMARY
As continued from page 71
to serve: Before serving, heat your gravy boat... as
Catherine says in the bush... the food won't get any
warmer! Squeeze the juice from the caramelised
lemons over the chicken when serving and also
squeeze the roasted garlic heads and use them as a
condiment. Dijon mustard is also great. SERVES 6-8

TIP: WHAT TO DO WITH THE LEFT OVERS (if any!)
1. The carcass is always good for making homemade
stock, which you can then use to make chicken,
mushroom & leek risotto.
2. The carcass is also good for making soup. Add
two turnips, two carrots, one leek and some celery
and Italian parsley and enough water to cover it.
Boil hard for an hour and season with salt and black
pepper to taste. Strain and add the remaining white
meat and some potato gnocchi and Italian parsley.
3. Shred the white meat and mix into a tzatsiki (Greek
yoghurt, grated drained cucumber, garlic and lemon
juice) and scoop into flatbreads or in wraps with
shredded iceberg lettuce and mint.
4. Take the potatoes and drizzle them with olive oil & more
fresh lemon juice & coarse sea salt & black pepper to
revive them. Makes a Greek roast potato salad!

ADDITIONAL CAPTIONS
pg 66 (L-R) 1. Cape country table from
Catherine's friend, Hannes Zaaiman 2. Catherine
in the mix with her cheesecake 3. Catherine's
one-of-a-kind indoor braai area

Visit www.unchartedafrica.com for more
information on Kleinefontein.

PHOTOGRAPHIC CONTRIBUTORS:
Tony Christie and Sean Laurenz

ADDITIONAL CAPTIONS
pg 88 (L-R) 1. The only woman living with Graeme
for the past 30 years! 2. Cookbook from Graeme's
favourite restaurant 3. Series of 3 "Giglee" prints
by Deryck Healey

PHOTOGRAPHIC CONTRIBUTOR:
Russel Wasserfall

OSTRICH RAGÙ LASAGNE:
FOR THE BÉCHAMEL SAUCE
As continued from page 113
40g butter • 40g flour • 600ml milk
• pinch of nutmeg

Melt the butter in a saucepan on a medium heat,
add the flour and stir around for 1-2 minutes to
cook it off. Then slowly start adding the milk while
whisking furiously. Add the nutmeg and turn up the
heat. When it comes to the boil, reduce the heat to a
simmer and keep stirring the sauce until it thickens,
then set aside.

no man in the world has more courage than the man who can stop after eating one peanut.
CHANNING POLLOCK

DOZZA'S BEEF WELLINGTON:
As continued from page 118
Transfer the cooled fillet to a wooden board, cut off the string and pat dry with kitchen paper. Spread half the mushroom pâté over one side of the beef. Lay the Parma ham on clingfilm, with slices overlapping. Put the beef on to the ham, mushroom-side down. Spread the remaining mushroom mixture over the beef, then fold over the rest of the Parma ham, wrapping it around the sides to make sure it is all covered. Wrap tightly in clingfilm and refrigerate for 20 minutes. Heat the oven to 220°C and unroll the pastry onto a lightly floured surface, using one piece as the base and saving the other piece to cover the top of the fillet. Prick the pastry lightly all over with a fork, and transfer the base to a baking tray lined with a silicone mat. Remove the clingfilm from the beef, put it in the middle of the pastry base and brush all around it with the egg wash. Flop the other piece of pastry over the top and press it down lightly to seal around the edges of the beef. Cut off all the extra pieces, leaving a little strip around the perimeter of the beef. Put in the fridge for 10 minutes or until ready to cook. Brush with more beaten egg and decorate with pastry leaves. Brush again with the eggwash and bake for 15 minutes, then turn down to 200°C and cook for a further 30 minutes for rare to medium rare. Leave to stand for 10 minutes before cutting. SERVES 6

ADDITIONAL CAPTIONS
pg 106 (L-R) 1. A good cook can never have too many utensils! 2. Brandon's early experiments with Champagne cork chairs... Prost! 3. Tea cosy knitted by Nikki's cousin-in-law, Guz.

pg 116 (L-R) 1. Special Royal Albert Bone China tea set originally owned by Brandon's mom, Denise, who lovingly gave it to Nikki. 2. Nicknamed "Pink Flamingo" by Brandon's folks for her very pink dress sense, Nikki has more in common with this steel cut-out then one might think! 3. Nikki's repertoire of German cooking includes knackwursts and potato salad... delish!

pg 120 (L-R) 1. Operation "Alpine wall mural" successfully completed by Bond who safely (& begrudgingly) carried the wallpaper all around Europe. 2. Their old-fashioned red telephone, which is apparently quite tiring to use when dialling cellphone numbers... 3. Let's do the time-warp agaaaain!

Russel and Camilla

PHOTOGRAPHIC CONTRIBUTOR:
Russel Wasserfall

ADDITIONAL CAPTIONS
pg 140 (L-R) 1. Debut cookbook, *The Farm Kitchen*, written by Russel & Camilla's mom 2. Shiitake mushrooms being prepped for the roast fillet 3. Camilla doing all the dirty work, for once, as I enthusiastically supervise.

PHOTOGRAPHIC CONTRIBUTOR:
Mark Lanning

ADDITIONAL CAPTIONS
pg 164 (L-R) 1. Surprise anniversary gift from Alex painted by their favourite artist, Annet Ellis. 2. Meet a member of the family, "Kost" man (meaning "broom" in English), by Miranda Du Toit. 3. Proudly South African.

PHOTOGRAPHIC CONTRIBUTORS:
Russel Wasserfall and Tony Christie

FOR THE WORLD'S BEST COLESLAW:
As continued from page 182
½ cup (125ml) red wine vinegar • 2t honey • ½ small head red cabbage, very thinly sliced and core discarded • ½ small head green cabbage, sliced very thinly and core discarded • ½ red onion, sliced thinly • 1 carrot, peeled & grated • 1 green pepper, deseeded & sliced very thinly • salt & freshly ground black pepper to taste • ½ cup (125ml) mayonnaise • a big pinch of cayenne pepper • ¼ cup (60ml) flat-leaf parsley

to make: In a small pan on a medium heat reduce the red wine vinegar by half, cool for five minutes and then stir in the honey until it dissolves. Combine the cabbages, onion, carrot and green pepper in a large bowl and pour the vinegar dressing over it. Toss well to combine. Season with salt and pepper and then - this bit is important - let it sit for 15 minutes to let the flavours combine. Toss with your hands every now and then. Finally, add the mayonnaise, cayenne pepper and parsley, toss well and season to taste. Dijon mustard is also great. SERVES 6

ADDITIONAL CAPTIONS
pg 180 (L-R) 1. Kate's best view is from her terrace in Tamboerskloof 2. Fresh ingredients from Kate's terrace pots 3. Just out the box, folks!

PHOTOGRAPHIC CONTRIBUTOR:
Tony Christie

RED PEPPER & YOGHURT DIP:
As continued from page 196
1 small jar (290g) red pepper relish • ½ cup (125ml) thick Greek yoghurt • salt & pepper to taste

to make: This is the easiest thing in the world to prepare. Mix a small jar of red pepper relish (available at most supermarkets) with about ½ cup thick Greek yoghurt. Season to taste and serve with the warm kibbeh. SERVES 6

HARISSA:
As continued from page 200
Traditionally served with couscous, bread and eggs, but it gives a great little kick to any dish. Make your own, it's really worth it.

1 large red bell pepper, deseeded, roasted, peeled & chopped • 200g fresh red chillies, deseeded & chopped roughly (wear gloves!) • 3t (level) cumin seeds, ground • 3t (level) caraway seeds, ground • 2t (level) smoked Spanish paprika • 4 garlic cloves • 1T tomato purée • 1T red wine vinegar • ½t black pepper, ground • 1t salt (or more to taste) • 5T extra virgin olive oil

to make: Whizz all the above ingredients together until you have a slightly coarse paste. Store in the fridge with a thin layer of olive oil to cover so it stays fresh. (Stored like this, it will keep for a few weeks in the fridge.)

ADDITIONAL CAPTIONS
pg 202 (L-R) 1. Theresa-Anne Mackintosh oil painting on canvas 2. Zulu teething beads from their beach cottage in Umkhomaas 3. Ruth's collection of vintage bowls & her favourite flowers, orchids, on her dressing table.

PHOTOGRAPHIC CONTRIBUTOR:
Tony Christie

ADDITIONAL CAPTIONS
pg 220 (L-R) 1. True collectors of curiosities will appreciate Greg & Roché's genuine ostrich foot lamp 2. The spacious dining room 3. A Guruth & Bonetti quirky lamp on their bedside table.

PHOTOGRAPHIC CONTRIBUTOR:
Tony Christie

ADDITIONAL CAPTIONS
pg 250 (L-R) 1. The neglected mountain bike 2. Cathy, Clint's maid, arranges his clothes by colour… strange but true! 3. A poster from Cobra's vintage travel collection.

What were you looking for?

SIDE DISHES & SALADS

AVO, PRAWN & FETA WITH SMOKED PAPRIKA MAYO, **239**
CITRUS SALAD WITH GRILLED DUCK BREAST, **135**
OLIVIEH SALAD (IRANIAN CHICKEN SALAD), **158**
OPA'S POTATO SALAD, **108**
PINK GRAPEFRUIT SALAD WITH MANDARIN & FRESH COCONUT, **238**
POACHED CHICKEN SALAD WITH ROCKET & POMEGRANATE SEEDS, **239**
RED PEPPER & PRESERVED LEMON SALAD, **197**
ROAST PEPPER SALAD, **138**
THE WORLD'S BEST COLESLAW, **182 / 263** (ADD)

DESSERTS

ALMOND CAKE WITH FRESH CHERRIES, **148**
BANANA BUTTERMILK PANCAKES, **65**
CHERRY CLAFOUTIS, **98**
CRANBERRY JELLY & LIQUORICE ICE-CREAM, **229**
CRÊPES AUX COINTREAU (COINTREAU PANCAKES), **47**
CHOCOLATE CHEESECAKE, **75**
FAR BRETON CAKE, **45**
GRAPEFRUIT AND ROSEWATER JELLY, **123**
GRANADILLA TART, **186**
HALVA ICE-CREAM, **204**
HEISSE LIEBE (HOT LOVE), **124**
HONEY PHYLLO PASTRY BISCUITS, **205**
HOT CROSS BUNS, **60**
MARQUISE AU CHOCOLAT, **50**
MERINGUES, **41**
MUM'S LEMON MERINGUE PIE, **122**
ORANGE CHIFFON CUPCAKES WITH GRANADILLA FROSTING, **27**
PARFAIT AUX FRAISES (STRAWBERRY PARFAIT), **44**
ROSE-PETAL POACHED PEARS WITH PISTACHIO NUT BRITTLE, **204**
STEWED FIGS IN RED WINE, **74**
STRAWBERRY ICE-CREAM, **95**
TARTE AUX PRUNES ET AUX AMANDES (PLUM & ALMOND TART), **40**
TARTE TATIN (CARAMELISED APPLE TART), **38**
TOASTED ENGLISH MUFFINS WITH MASCARPONE & CARAMEL, **61**

DRINKS

LIMONCELLO, **86**
MARGARITA PIPETTE SHOOTERS, **253**
PINK MARTINI, **125**

Thanks*

to all the Shiny Happy People
who opened their door to me

CREATIVE DIRECTOR	Neil Roake
PHOTOGRAPHY	Tony Christie, Russel Wasserfall, Mark Lanning, Adriaan Louw, Mark Williams, Sean Laurénz, Ray Du Toit & Michael Jnr Bowles
SENIOR DESIGNER & STYLIST	Kelly Chrystal
DESIGNER	Camilla Grobler
SENIOR COPYWRITER	Mark Beckett
COPYWRITER & JOURNALIST	Janna Turner
ILLUSTRATOR	Greg Davies
COVER CONCEPT & TYPOGRAPHY	Scott Robertson
PRODUCTION	Jenna Geldenhuys & Katya Van Der Zanden

PRODUCED IN SOUTH AFRICA IN 2009 BY MODERN MUSEUM PUBLISHING
COPYRIGHT © NEIL ROAKE
PHOTOGRAPHS © TONY CHRISTIE, © RUSSEL WASSERFALL, © MARK LANNING, © ADRIAAN LOUW,
© RAY DU TOIT, © MICHAEL JNR BOWLES, © MARK WILLIAMS & © SEAN LAURÉNZ.
THE RIGHT OF NEIL ROAKE TO BE IDENTIFIED AS AUTHOR OF THIS WORK HAS BEEN ASSERTED BY HIM
IN ACCORDANCE WITH SOUTH AFRICAN LAW.
ISBN: 978-0620446815 ALL RIGHTS RESERVED
jenny@modernmuseum.co.za
P.O. Box 1724, Hillcrest, 3650, KZN, South Africa
www.modernmuseum.co.za
Printed by Tien Wah Press Pte Ltd.